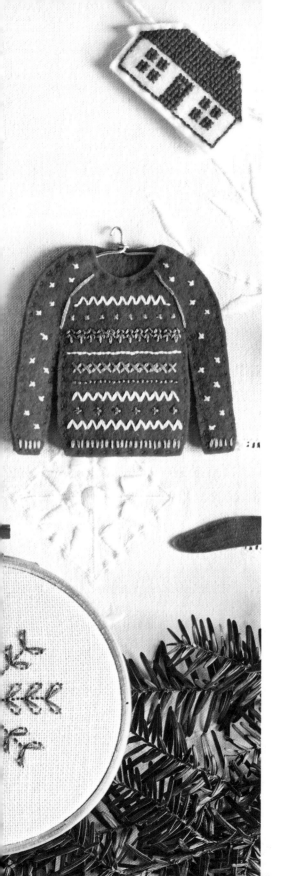

Contents

A hearty ho...ho...ho...

...to you all at this most wonderful time of year. I'll let you in on a little secret: Christmas is my happy place. At the first sign of cold weather, you will find me curled under a blanket with my *Home Alone* soundtrack on repeat, wishing for snow. Add in a slew of stitching projects to keep idle hands busy and you have the very definition of festive joy. With that in mind, I have designed a collection full of Christmas goodness to help you festoon your home and spread some seasonal delight. With a little time and love, you can create ornaments so unique and beautiful that they will become family heirlooms – keepsakes to be treasured by future generations.

I am best known for my cross stitch designs, and you will find a fair few of those within these pages, but sometimes even I crave a little variety, so in this book I will also introduce you to counted thread work. This is not a million miles away from the straightforward little crosses you are used to – in fact a number of the stitches are variations of traditional cross stitch – so if you can do one, you will have no problem with the other.

I have grouped the projects into sections, each with a distinctive style, but they are designed to be mixed and matched ad infinitum. Choose thread and fabric colours to match your colour scheme and infuse your own personality into each and every stitch. Use scarlet thread for the Advent Tree Bag-lets, for example, and they will find a home in even the most traditional scheme, or stitch the Jumbo Christmas Sock-ing in a neon palette and it will delight the edgiest hipster in town.

My designs are meant as a blueprint to help you build up your own enviable collection of handmade Christmas decorations for posterity. Most of them, like the Perpetual 'Paper' Chains for example, can be broken down into manageable stitching chunks – add a little each year and before you know it you will have the best-dressed home in all the land. So without further ado I shall let you turn the page and hop to it. May your hand-stitched Christmas be supremely merry and bright!

Delilah

x

{FABRIC}

Counted Thread Fabric

Counted embroidery is most commonly worked on evenweave fabrics such as linen or cotton evenweave, or on blockweaves such as aida and waste canvas. Evenweaves and blockweaves are woven with the same number of threads in the warp and the weft, meaning that the holes between the woven threads form a grid of squares (like graph paper) that correspond to the pattern you are following.

Aida and waste canvas are woven in blocks that create very obvious squares to work on, making them perfect for beginners, whereas stitching over two threads at a time forms the squares on cotton evenweave or linen. Stitching on linen or evenweave takes a little more thought, but the finish is far nicer.

Evenweave fabrics come in different 'thread counts'. The higher the count, the finer the fabric and the smaller your stitches will be. Evenweaves are counted by the number of individual threads per inch, whereas blockweaves are counted by the number of blocks per inch, so stitches worked on a 14-count aida will be the same size as those worked on a 28-count linen, because the linen is worked over two threads at a time. Each project specifies the type of fabric I have used, but feel free to substitute a different fabric of the same thread count if you prefer, so, for example, a 32-count evenweave could be substituted for a 16-count aida.

Felt

I have used felt for many of the small ornament projects in this book as its raw edges do not fray when cut, so it can be turned into small, fiddly shapes very easily. However since felt is not woven, you will need to use waste canvas to count your stitches onto it (see below).

IMPORTANT: I specify thick (1mm/^{1}/$_{16}$in+) 100% wool felt in the material lists because it must be strong enough to support the stitches and withstand the strain of removing waste canvas. If you use a wool-viscose mix or acrylic felt it will not hold your embroidery well and it is likely to shrink significantly and lose shape when the canvas is removed. It is easy to source 100% wool felt, especially online (see Suppliers, page 79).

Using waste canvas

Waste canvas can be used to work counted stitches on non-evenweave fabrics without a visible grid to stitch over. The stitch diagrams on pages 9 and 12–15 are shown being worked on waste canvas.

Cut the waste canvas to the same size as your felt and mark its centre with a pin (step 1).

Tack the waste canvas in place on top of the felt all around the edge, using a length of waste thread and a loose running stitch (step 2).

Work your embroidery stitches through both layers of fabric. When the design is finished, remove the

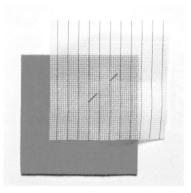

STEP 1

STEP 2

tacking stitches and *lightly* spray the waste canvas with water to loosen the threads (over-wetting will soak the felt underneath and make the waste canvas difficult to remove; it is best to spray just a little to begin with, then re-spray as needed). While the waste canvas is damp, use tweezers or a small pair of pliers to pull out one thread at a time until it is all gone (step 3).

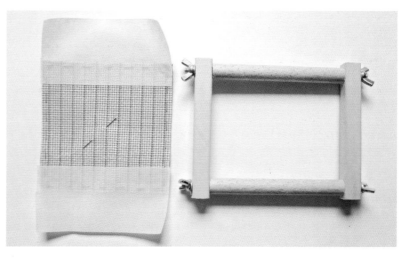

STEP 3

{THREAD}

The majority of the projects in this book use stranded cotton embroidery thread. Its six strands are loosely twisted together so that they can be easily separated for stitching with different thicknesses. Each charted pattern lists the number of strands you will need to use to create the same effect on the project fabric; feel free to increase or reduce the number of strands, or to substitute another thread if you prefer.

I have also used Kreinik metallic braid. It comes in different weights depending on what you are stitching and, unlike stranded cotton, you do not separate it but stitch with the whole thread at once. It is best to keep your thread lengths slightly shorter than usual when working with metallics to minimise fraying and knotting.

{NEEDLES}

Embroidery needles come in many different shapes and sizes, but generally have one thing in common: a large eye through which you can thread multiple strands at the same time. Working on evenweave and blockweave fabrics, you will need a blunt tapestry needle that will slide easily through the holes in the fabric without splitting the threads on either side. For working on

waste canvas on top of another fabric, such as felt, you will need a sharp embroidery needle to pierce through the base fabric. Details of the best needle to use are given in the materials list for each project.

{HOOPS & FRAMES}

It is not essential to use an embroidery hoop or frame when you stitch, but more often than not I opt to do so, especially if I am stitching onto soft linen or cotton evenweave fabrics as I find it helps to keep the tension of my stitches even; without one, I find my hand aches from holding the fabric

taut and stitching at the same time. There are many different types of hoops and frames available, but for almost all of the projects in this book I have used mini no-sew frames.

Whether or not you choose to use a hoop or frame, and which you opt for, really is a matter of personal preference. In actual fact many of the small felt projects in this book can be stitched perfectly easily without a hoop or a frame as the combination of the thick felt and the waste canvas creates a rigid base to stitch onto.

Mini No-Sew Frames

These are miniature versions of traditional rolling tapestry frames; they come with different sizes of mix and match rollers and side bars, which are perfect for small projects. As the name suggests, you do not have to sew your work into the frame; instead, thick masking tape is used to attach the fabric to the rollers, which is plenty strong enough for working the small projects in this book. As the fabric only needs to fill the length of the side bars, less fabric is required than if you were using a hoop.

To fix fabric into a mini no-sew frame, cut two pieces of wide masking tape to the width of the fabric and stick along opposite ends.

Attach the overlap of each piece of masking tape to its respective roller.

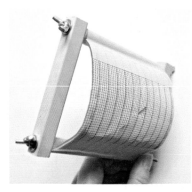

Finally, roll the excess fabric around the rollers until the fabric is taut and then tighten the four wing nuts to hold it in place.

Embroidery Hoops
Embroidery hoops are used for the Mistletoe Snowflake Hoops, both to work, then to frame the finished designs. If you choose to use an

embroidery hoop when working other projects, please remember that for many of the smallest patterns you will need to use more fabric to fit the same project into the whole hoop than when working on a mini no-sew frame.

To fix your fabric into a hoop, first mark the centre point with a pin; loosen the screw at the top of the hoop and separate the two rings. Place the inner ring on a flat surface and lay the fabric, centred, on top of it. Place the outer ring on top of the fabric and push it down to trap the fabric in between. Tighten the screw on the outer ring; pull on the excess fabric around the edge to give you a taut, drum-like circle of fabric in the middle.

{OTHER EQUIPMENT}

Embroidery scissors: A good, sharp pair of small pointed scissors is essential. Keep for snipping threads and quick trimming jobs.

Measuring tape: For accurate measuring, this is a necessity.

Fabric shears & pinking shears: For cutting larger pieces of fabric or finishing edges when making up projects. Use for fabric cutting only to keep them nice and sharp.

Rotary cutter: A supremely sharp cutting tool that should always be used with a metal ruler and self-healing cutting mat; this will vastly reduce the time it takes to make up projects like the Advent Tree Bag-lets and Perpetual 'Paper' Chain.

Paper scissors & scalpel: For cutting out paper templates and plastic.

Pins: While any decent dressmaking pins will do the job, glass-headed pins are less likely to get lost in the fabric.

Tailor's chalk: For marking around templates onto fabric; it leaves a distinct line that shows up against dark fabrics and will brush away easily if needs be.

Hand sewing needle & sewing thread: While a sewing machine will make a few of these projects faster, it is not essential; I chose to stitch most things by hand for greater control. A sharp sewing needle is best for fine sewing threads.

Iron & terry towel: Always press your project before making up – it makes the world of difference. Place your embroidery face down over a folded terry towel and iron it on the *reverse*.

Tracing paper: Essential for making transparent project templates. It can also be used for marking up charts: use washi tape to hold the paper in place over the chart and track your stitching progress over the top.

Red pen or pencil: For marking where you're up to on a chart, making notes and drawing out templates.

Point turner: Often made of bone or plastic, this is a flat stick with a gently rounded point at one end, used for pushing out corners when making up projects. You could also use a large knitting needle or the lid of a pen – anything with a blunt point will do the trick.

Counted Embroidery: The Basics

Counted embroidery, encompassing counted cross stitch and counted thread techniques, is based on a set of simple stitches that can be picked up really quickly. The projects in this book are brilliant for beginners, while being interesting and varied enough to provide instant gratification for advanced stitchers. The basic techniques outlined here will stand you in good stead whatever your level.

{READING COUNTED EMBROIDERY CHARTS}

All types of counted embroidery are worked from charts that are based on a grid system: the grid lines either represent the threads in your fabric (for counted thread charts) or the stitched areas between those threads (for cross stitch charts). You will find examples of both types of chart throughout the book.

Each chart throughout the book is labelled as either 'Cross Stitch' or 'Counted Thread', and the following examples will show you how to read each style. Occasionally, both cross stitch and counted thread stitches are used on the same chart and in these instances I have chosen the most appropriate type of chart for the majority of stitches in the design, and the stitches in the chart will be displayed and aligned to fit the chosen style.

Cross Stitch Charts

Counted cross stitch patterns use only one type of stitch (crosses) in the same size throughout so there is no need to distinguish between different stitch techniques. However, they do often use multiple colours, which would be difficult to tell apart on a chart if they were shown as thin stitch lines. For this reason cross stitch charts show blocks of colour or symbols in a grid: the points where the lines cross in the grid correspond to the holes in the fabric, so you are counting the number of holes. Fractional stitches (such as the four corners of the shape below) are shown as a partially completed block in the grid.

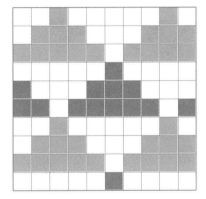

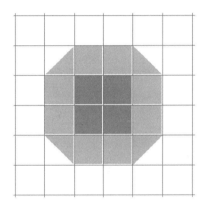

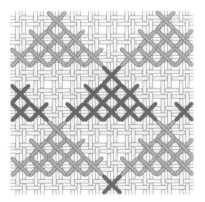

Counted Thread Charts

Counted thread designs use a variety of different stitches that are shown as thin lines placed in between the grid lines, to enable you to distinguish the stitches from the grid lines. This effectively means that each grid line represents a thread of the fabric, so you are counting the number of threads you cross (hence the name 'counted thread') as opposed to the number of holes as in counted cross stitch. This can take a bit of getting used to if you are accustomed to working from counted cross stitch charts, but it actually makes more sense as the grid is a more direct representation of the fabric's anatomy.

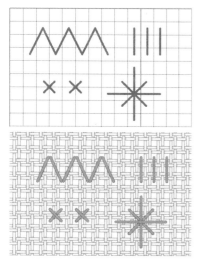

{STARTING TO STITCH}

Finding Your Start Point

Counted embroidery charts are not generally printed to scale, often being larger than the finished stitched design so that you can clearly tell the individual stitches apart. To ensure your stitching ends up in the right place on your fabric, work from the centre of the pattern outwards.

First find the centre of your fabric: fold it in half one way, open it out again and then fold it in half the other way, gently pressing along the middle of each fold to find the point where they cross.

Once you have found the centre point, mark it with a pin or your needle until you are ready to begin stitching.

The centre point of each charted design is marked with intersecting lines on the cross stitch charts and with a contrasting coloured dot on the counted thread charts, and this centre point corresponds to the centre of the fabric. Pick the start of a row or section of stitches close to the centre point on the chart and count the number of holes or threads from the centre to this spot, making a note of this distance on the chart. Now count the same number of holes or threads away from the centre point of your fabric to find the place where you will make your first stitch. (Remember, if working on linen or cotton evenweave you will need to double the number.)

Preparing the Thread

Cut a length of thread about as long as your arm. If standard six-stranded cotton is being used, the chart notes will specify the number of strands required. To separate strands, find the end of one strand and hold it firmly between your thumb and forefinger. With your other hand, loosely hold the rest of the strands together and push them down while you pull the single strand up and out of the thread. Straighten out the remaining strands and repeat until you are left with six separate strands. Now take the required number of strands and line them up together to form a single thread that is the right thickness to stitch the pattern with.

Knot-free Stitching

It helps to keep the back of your stitching almost as neat as the front: you will often need to go through the same hole multiple times and if you have lots of knots and tangled threads on the back of your work, you will struggle to do this. To secure the start of your thread without a knot, the following methods are best.

Away waste knot start
This method can be used to secure threads made up of any number of strands. It uses a temporary knot to hold the end of the thread out of the way while you work the first few stitches. Tie a double knot in the thread end; bring the needle down through the fabric about 10cm (4in) away from the stitching start point, to leave the knot sitting at the front. Make your first few stitches, then snip off the temporary knot and thread the loose end behind four or five completed stitches on the back of the work before trimming off the excess.

AWAY WASTE KNOT START

Knotless loop start
This is my favourite method, but it only works if you are using an even number of strands (2, 4 or 6).

To stitch with four strands using this method, for example, take two long strands of thread, line them up together as usual and then fold the length in half so that you have a single length of thread that is four strands thick with four loose strands at one end and a loop at the other.

Thread the end with the loose strands through the eye of the needle. Bring the needle up through the underside of the fabric at the stitching start point, leaving a few centimetres of thread (the end with the loop) underneath. Put the needle back

KNOTLESS LOOP START

through the surface of the fabric to form the first stitch, and then through the middle of the loop that has been left at the back. Once the thread is pulled all the way through the loop it will be fixed to the fabric – with no need for a knot.

Finishing a Thread
When you only have 10cm (4in) or so of thread left, run the needle underneath four or five completed stitches on the back of the fabric to secure it without a knot, then neatly snip off the loose end.

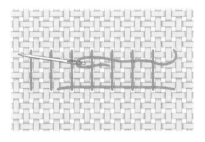

PROJECT ASSEMBLY: FINISHING ON FELT

To fasten the end of a thread when making up projects, first make a couple of backstitches. Next push the needle in between the layers of felt, then pull it back out again, bringing the last of the thread with it, and trim off the excess.

Stitch Directory

{STRAIGHT STITCH}

Straight stitch joins two points on your fabric together (A to B) in a single stitch. They can be any length and face any direction, and appear in charts as solid straight lines.

To make a straight stitch, come up through the fabric at A and back down at B. The stitches can be combined to make complex patterns. When working

on evenweave fabrics, keep the threads on the back running along the same paths as the stitches on the front to

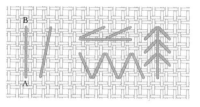

prevent show through. Keep the stitch tension fairly tight as longer stitches will flop about if they are too slack.

{RUNNING STITCH}

Running stitch is shown as dashed lines on a chart and is worked as a continuous line of stitches in sequence.

To work a running stitch, come up through the fabric at A, back down at B, up again at C, down at D, and so on. The length of the

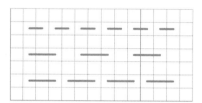

individual stitches and the distance between them can vary, so be

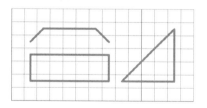

sure to refer to the chart you are working from for the specifics.

{BACKSTITCH}

Backstitch, like straight stitch, is also shown as a solid straight line on a chart, but the difference is that it is worked as a sequence of lots of little stitches. (The chart annotations or notes will clearly distinguish between the two stitches.)

To work backstitch, come up through the fabric at A and down at B; come up again at C, then back down at D, where the previous stitch ended. Continue in this way – forward

then back, forward then back – for the length of the line on the chart. Backstitch can turn corners and will work along any line – horizontal, vertical or at a 45 degree angle.

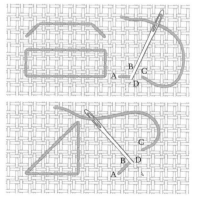

{CROSS STITCH}

Cross stitch is one of the most popular of counted stitches. Many designs are made up of cross stitch only and on a counted cross stitch chart each stitch will be shown as a filled square (see right and page 9). When combined with other stitches on a counted thread chart, cross stitches will be represented with an X (see below right) and may be worked at different scales.

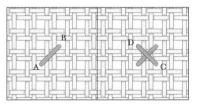

Working a Single Cross Stitch

Cross stitch is essentially just two diagonal stitches that cross over each other to form an X shape. To work a single cross stitch, come up through the fabric at A and make a diagonal stitch to go down at B; come up at C and make a diagonal stitch to go down at D, to complete the X.

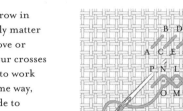

Working Cross Stitch in Rows

When a pattern contains blocks of multiple cross stitches in the same colour, it is generally quicker to work these in rows. First complete all of the half stitches in a row by making a series of single diagonal stitches (A to B, C to D, and so on).

When you get to the end of the row, work back to the start to cross the stitches just made (I to J, K to L, and so on).

Next, move on to the row below or above and complete that row in the same way. It doesn't really matter if you work the next row above or below, or even which way your crosses overlap, but it is important to work all of your stitches in the same way, so if, for example, you decide to work your first diagonal half stitch leaning to the left and the top of the cross leaning to the right, keep it up all the way through the pattern.

Working Fractional Cross Stitches

Small cross stitch patterns sometimes contain fractional (half or three-quarter) stitches in order to create more detail in the design. Half stitches are shown as short diagonal lines and three-quarter stitches as partially completed blocks, leaning in the direction of the finished stitch.

For three-quarter stitches one of the diagonals is cut short, ending in the centre instead of the opposite corner, so they are best worked on linen, cotton evenweave or waste canvas as you will need access to a hole in the centre of the stitch, which does not exist with aida.

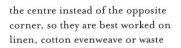

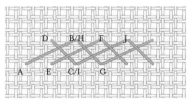

{LONG ARMED CROSS STITCH}

This cross stitch variation uses a longer first stitch and a series of overlaps to create a strikingly different effect. Work A to B, C to D, E to F, G to H, and so on.

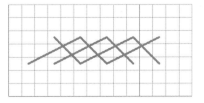

{HERRINGBONE STITCH}

A simple, open stitch pattern of overlapping stitches: work A to B, C to D, E to F, G to H, and so on.

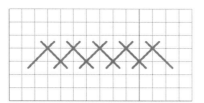 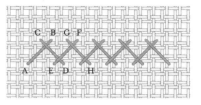

{CLOSED HERRINGBONE STITCH}

Worked in the same sequence as regular herringbone stitch, all of the lines join up to create a dense texture. This technique uses a lot of thread so start with a reasonable length.

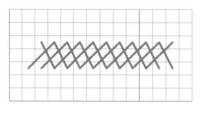 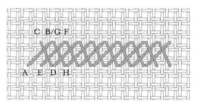

{UPRIGHT CROSS STITCH}

A very simple stitch where a horizontal stitch is worked (A to B) and then a vertical stitch (C to D) to form an upright cross stitch.

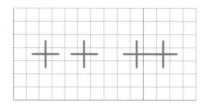 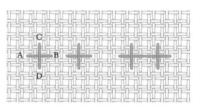

{DOUBLE STRAIGHT CROSS STITCH}

Work an upright cross stitch, then work a regular cross stitch on top to create the pretty star effect.

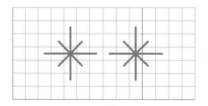 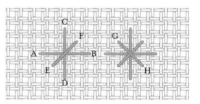

TIPS

◊ When working a series of stitches together, it is best to begin a stitch by bringing your needle up through a 'clean' hole (one with no stitches) as you are less likely to split existing stitches this way; pushing your needle back down through the fabric (front to reverse) when there are existing stitches in a hole rarely causes a problem.

◊ The scale and relative dimensions of many of these stitches can change depending on the charted design, so follow the chart carefully.

◊ With any crossed stitch, it doesn't matter whether you choose to work each stitch from A to B or B to A, but do layer the stitches in the same order each time to keep your work looking neat.

{SMYRNA STITCH}

When you work the diagonal (regular) cross stitch first, with a small upright cross stitch on top, more of a square star shape is made and a Smyrna stitch is created.

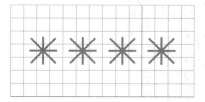 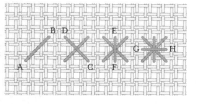

{ZIGZAG-HOLBEIN COMBO STITCH}

My twist on traditional Holbein stitch combines it with a zigzag line for a thoroughly modern feel. It is most effective when worked in two contrasting colours: start by stitching all of the first colour, then go back to the start and fill in the contrasting colour.

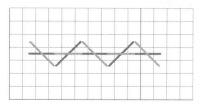 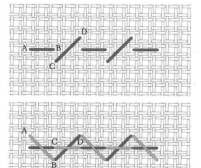

APPROXIMATE STITCH TIME

The quickest design in this book takes just 10 minutes to embroider, and none takes more than 3½ hours. Look out for the tree logo that accompanies each chart, which will give you an approximate stitch time (AST) for embroidering the design. Project assembly will take a little longer.

The Mini Sampler Stocking (pages 48–51) is a great project for trying out lots of counted thread embroidery stitches.

{ STYLISH & CHIC for sophisticates }

Snowy Forest Mittens

{MATERIALS}
FOR EACH MITTEN

14-count waste canvas, 15 x 20cm (6 x 8in)

Three pieces of thick (1mm/^{1}/16in+) cream or dark grey 100% wool felt, 15 x 20cm (6 x 8in) each

4m (13ft) stranded cotton embroidery thread in dark green (DMC 520) for cream felt or in cream (DMC ecru) for dark grey felt

Sharp embroidery needle, size 6

Embroidery scissors and pins

Water spray and tweezers

Cotton tape, 15cm (6in)

Sewing needle and thread to match felt colour

Tracing paper, pencil and paper scissors

Tailor's chalk

Mini no-sew frame (15cm/6in side bars and rollers) and masking tape (optional)

These sweet little mittens conjure thoughts of snow-covered cabins, lumberjacks and peaceful midwinter wanderings amidst towering trees. Fill them with treats to increase their appeal even further.

1.
Mark the centre of the waste canvas and attach it to one piece of the felt (see page 6). Tape the layered fabric into the frame if you are using one (see page 7).

2.
Following the chart on page 20, count outwards from the centre and using an away waste knot start (see page 10), stitch the design in rows, one section or motif at a time, using three strands of embroidery thread.

3.
When you have finished stitching, take the fabric out of the frame, unpick the tacking stitches and remove the waste canvas (see page 6).

4.
Make a tracing of the mitten template on page 78. Cut it out and use it to mark the mitten shape around the embroidery using tailor's chalk and centring the design. Cut out the mitten shape from the felt.

5.
Cut two more mitten shapes from the remaining two pieces of felt for the backing pieces. Take the piece of cotton tape and fold it in half to make a hanging loop. Pin it in between the embroidered mitten and one of the backing layers (I pinned mine at a slight angle so that the mitten would hang more naturally).

STEP 5

{SNOWY FOREST MITTENS CROSS STITCH CHART}

AST
2½ hrs

STITCHES USED
Cross Stitch

PATTERN SIZE
48 x 65 stitches

STITCHED SIZE
9 x 12cm (3½ x 4¾in)
on 14-ct waste canvas

THREAD
Stranded cotton, 3 strands,
dark green (DMC 520)
for cream felt
or
cream (DMC ecru) for grey felt

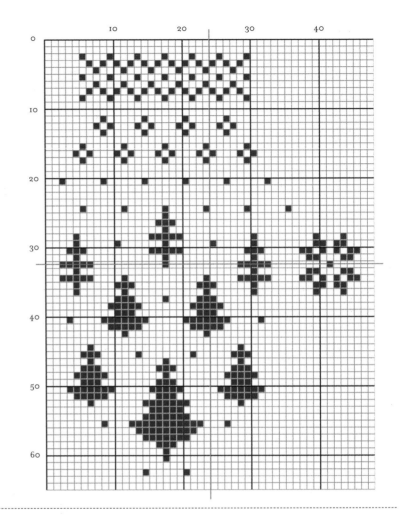

6.

Using a double thickness of sewing thread and a knotless loop start, stitch the two mitten shapes together with a small, neat running stitch close to the top edge only, making a few extra stitches back and forth over the hanging loop for extra strength.

STEP 6

7.

When you come to the end of the top edge, pick up the remaining mitten shape and layer it at the back of the joined together mitten shapes. As you go around the corner, begin to stitch

STEP 7

through the third layer too, so that you are now joining all three pieces of felt as you work your way down and around the edge of the mitten shape.

8.

Continue the running stitch all the way around the mitten shape until you get to the opposite corner of the top edge. The top is going to be left open to fill with treats, so make a couple of backstitches to secure the thread, before finishing off (see page 11).

Rosemary Wreath Alpha Tags

These stylish little gift tags are one of my favourite ever makes. They are incredibly quick to stitch and will lend an air of subtle sophistication to your gifts as they wait patiently under the Christmas tree. Paired up with brown paper, string and a sprig of seasonal foliage, they are the ultimate in simple elegance.

{MATERIALS}

FOR EACH TAG

14-count waste canvas, 10 x 10cm (4 x 4in)

Two pieces of thick (1mm/$\frac{1}{16}$in+) cream 100% wool felt, 10 x 10cm (4 x 4in) each

0.5m (20in) stranded cotton embroidery thread each in green (DMC 367) and black (DMC 310)

Sharp embroidery needle, size 6

Cream embroidery thread (DMC ecru) for making up

Embroidery scissors

Water spray and tweezers

String or twine for threading/ wrapping

Mini no-sew frame (10cm/4in side bars and rollers) and masking tape (optional)

TIPS

◊ *These tags would look lovely in white thread on a dark charcoal background, or stitched with glittering gold metallic thread if you have the patience for it.*

◊ *Thread the little discs along a length of ribbon to spell out 'Merry Christmas', or wrap larger gifts by spelling out an entire name.*

1.

Mark the centre of the waste canvas and attach it to one piece of the felt (see page 6). Tape the layered fabric into the frame if you are using one (see page 7).

2.

Following your chosen letter chart (see pages 23–25) and using two strands of stranded cotton and a knotless loop start (see page 10), count the number of holes out from the centre point to begin by stitching the black letter in the middle. When you come to the end of the letter (depending on which one you are stitching), there will often be no significant stitches to anchor the end of your thread behind, so it is best to temporarily bring it through to the front of the fabric to keep it out of the way until you have completed a little of the wreath.

3.

Move on to stitch the green wreath, again using a knotless loop start and two strands; once some of the wreath has been completed, take the black thread back through to the reverse and weave it through some of the green stitches before snipping off the excess. Continue to finish stitching the wreath.

4.

Remove the fabric from the frame, unpick the tacking stitches and remove the waste canvas (see page 6). Cut a circle around the wreath and use it

as a template to cut a matching piece of felt.

5.

Layer the two circles of felt together, right sides facing out. Using a double thickness of cream embroidery thread, begin with a knotless loop start and join the two layers of felt together with a small, neat running stitch close to the edge in two semi-circular arcs, leaving the middle section open for threading through the string. Secure the thread with a couple of backstitches before finishing off (see page 11).

STEP 5

6.

Thread the tag onto a piece of string (tweezers may make this easier) and wrap it around your parcel.

STEP 6

{ROSEMARY WREATH ALPHA TAGS COUNTED THREAD CHARTS}

FOR EACH LETTER

STITCHES USED
Straight Stitch

PATTERN SIZE
20 x 20 holes

STITCHED SIZE
3.5 x 3.5cm (1⅜ x 1⅜in)
on 14-ct waste canvas

THREAD
Stranded cotton,
2 strands, green (DMC 367)
and black (DMC 310)

EXTRA INFO
Charts marked with a red star
contain an irregularly placed letter
– one or more of its straight stitches
lies between two blocks in order to be
properly aligned within the wreath

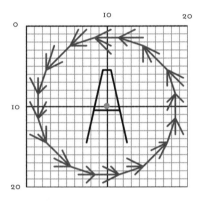

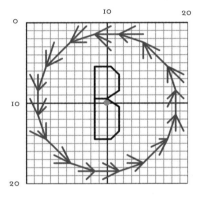

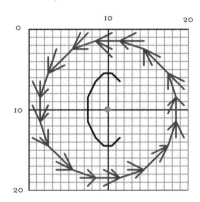

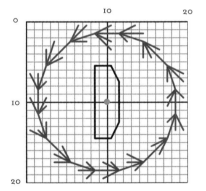

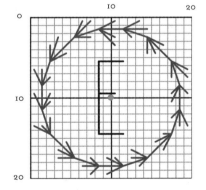

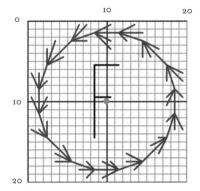

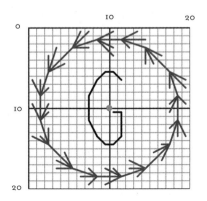

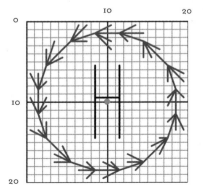

Rosemary Wreath Alpha Tags

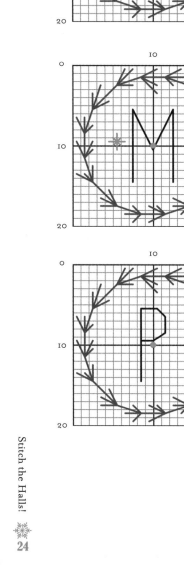
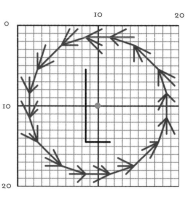
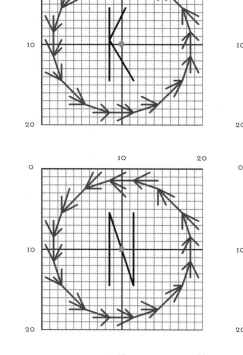
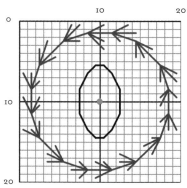
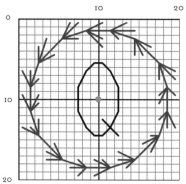
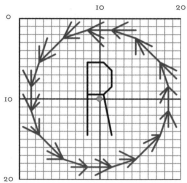

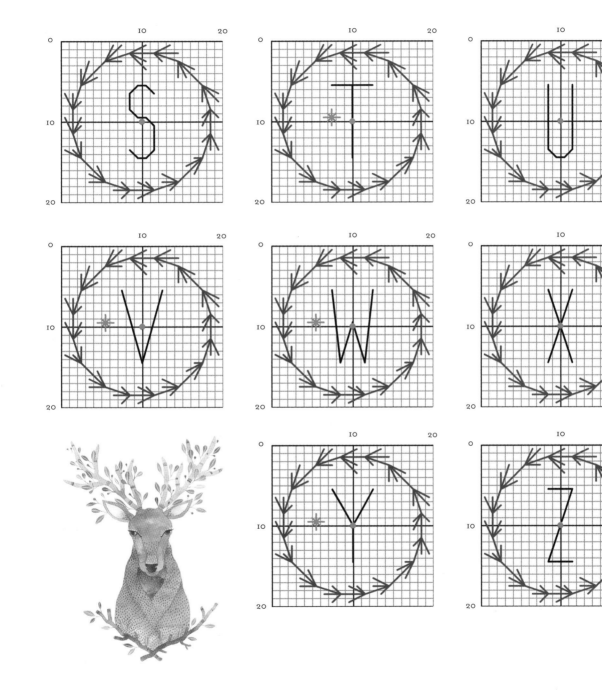

Polar Parade Bunting

{MATERIALS}

FOR EACH FLAG

32-count cream linen or cotton evenweave fabric, 20 x 20cm (8 x 8in)

Black cotton backing fabric, 20 x 20cm (8 x 8in)

3m (10ft) stranded cotton embroidery thread in black (DMC 310)

1.5m (5ft) Kreinik Very Fine Braid #4, shade 104C Colonial Gold

Tapestry needle, size 26

Embroidery scissors and pins

Tracing paper, pencil, paper scissors and tailor's chalk

Sewing machine or sewing needle and cream sewing thread

Rotary cutter, metal ruler and cutting mat (optional)

Mini no-sew frame (15cm/6in side bars and 23cm/9in rollers) and masking tape (optional)

Point turner (optional)

Although black and cream isn't known for being the most festive colour pairing, with its shimmering golden stars this bunting sums up exactly how I like my Christmas to look. With its fractional cross stitches and precision making up, this project is best suited to the advanced beginner or intermediate stitcher.

1.
Find the centre of your evenweave fabric and mark it with a pin (see page 10); fix it into the frame if you are using one (see page 7).

2.
Stitch your chosen design from the centre of the chart outwards (see pages 29–31 for charts), starting with the animal motif, using two strands of the black thread and working in rows.

3.
Next stitch the gold stars using a single thickness of the metallic thread – secure the end of the thread behind some nearby black stitches on the reverse to start and finish. You can carry the thread between each star on the back, but try to work the stars in sequence to prevent lots of very long, loose threads. The stars are supposed to look randomly placed so don't worry if your counting goes a little awry. When you have finished stitching, remove the fabric from its frame.

4.
Repeat steps 1–3 until you have the number of embroidered triangles you want for your bunting.

5.
Before you begin making up, iron all of your pieces of embroidery face down over a folded terry towel to remove any creases.

FOR MAKING FLAGS INTO BUNTING

To make the flags into a length of bunting with a total of six flags, you will also require a 160cm (5¼ft) length of 2.5-cm (1-in) wide cream bias tape. Increase the length of the tape if you wish to add more flags.

6.

Trace the triangular template from page 77 onto a piece of tracing paper, making sure to transfer the markings too. Cut the template out and line it up over each piece of your embroidery in turn so that the stitched parts fall inside the dotted seam line. Mark around the edge of the template with a pencil and cut out each shape.

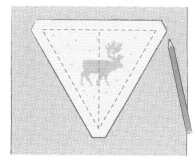

STEP 6

7.

Use the template and tailor's chalk to mark and cut out an identical shape from black backing fabric for each of your embroidered triangles (a rotary cutter and metal ruler will be quicker and more precise, and using black backing fabric means that the threads between the stars do not show through on the front).

TIPS

◊ *Try mixing up the monochrome effect by stitching some of the triangles with cream thread on black fabric and then alternating the two along the bunting.*

◊ *Use the individual patterns to make triangular shaped stuffed ornaments for your tree.*

8.

Take an embroidered triangle and a black backing triangle and pin together with right sides facing. Sew along each side edge with a 1cm (⅜in) seam, pivoting the fabric around the machine needle at the bottom point and securing loose ends with a few backstitches. Leave the top edge open. (If hand stitching, a backstitch or close running stitch is best.)

9.

Carefully trim the excess fabric to within 5mm (¼in) of each seam. Trimming the seams will reduce the bulk on the inside to give a much neater finish and a nice sharp point when the flag is turned through, but take care not to cut so close that the seams unravel.

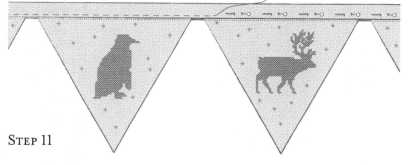

STEP 11

STEP 12

10.

Turn each flag to the right side and carefully push out the point with a point turner (or similar blunt poking tool). Press flat with the embroidered side face down over a terry towel to protect the stitches.

11.

Once all the flags are made, make them up into a string of bunting. Fold the bias tape in half widthways and press all along the seam. Gently fold the pressed tape in half lengthways to find the centre, then arrange your triangles along the tape from the centre outwards, aligning the top edges with the pressed fold and pinning in place. Sew all along the length of the bias tape close to the bottom edge (use a running stitch if sewing by hand).

12.

Follow the diagram on the left to fold the ends of the tape to hide the raw edges, and sew closed with a small line of stitching.

{POLAR PARADE BUNTING CROSS STITCH CHARTS}

FOR EACH FLAG

STITCHES USED
Cross Stitch,
Three-Quarter Cross Stitch,
Double Straight Cross Stitch (stars)

PATTERN SIZE
76 x 63 stitches

STITCHED SIZE
12 x 10cm (4¾ x 4in)
on 32-ct cotton evenweave/linen

THREAD
Stranded cotton, 2 strands,
black (DMC 310); Kreinik Very Fine
Braid #4, shade 104C Colonial Gold,
single thickness

EXTRA INFO
The triangular lines are not meant
to be stitched, but just show the shape
of the bunting

{PENGUIN}

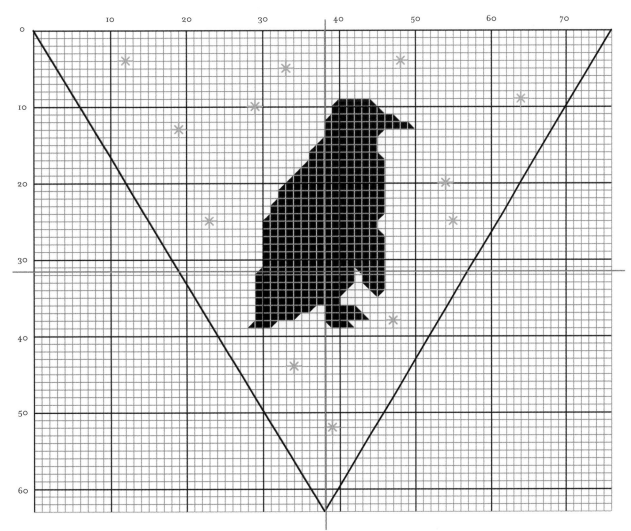

AST
3½ hrs

{POLAR BEAR}

AST
3½ hrs

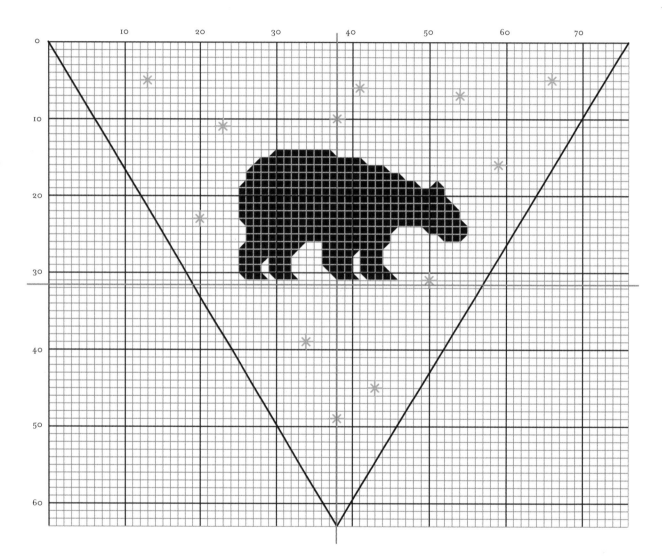

{REINDEER}

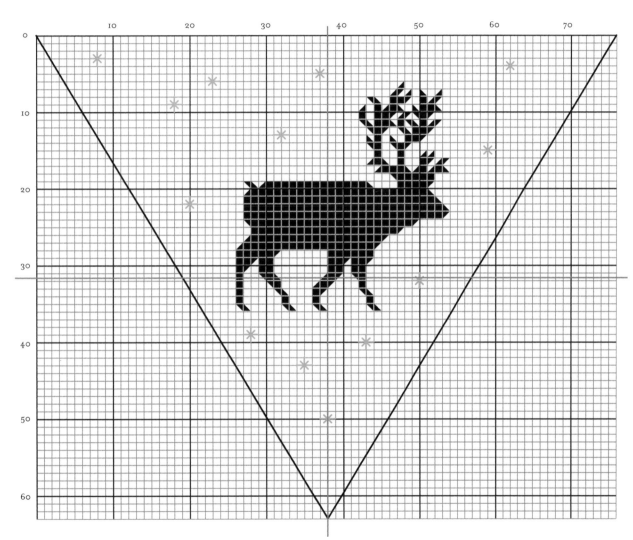

Mistletoe Snowflake Hoops

{MATERIALS}
FOR 3 HOOPS

Three pieces of 28-count cream linen or cotton evenweave fabric, 20 x 20cm (8 x 8in) each

Three pieces of cream cotton backing fabric (craft cotton or calico), 20 x 20cm (8 x 8in) each

Stranded cotton embroidery threads: 4m (13ft) in black (DMC 310) and 3m (10ft) in green (DMC 367)

4m (13ft) Kreinik Fine Braid #8, shade 104C Colonial Gold

Wooden hoops: one 13cm (5in) and two 10cm (4in)

Tapestry needle, size 24

Embroidery scissors

Strong craft glue

Mistletoe and snowflakes are Christmas stalwarts, so why not combine the two? Each of these simple hoops can be stitched in under an hour and they make a lovely wall display when grouped in a cluster. Ideal for beginners, they use just two easy stitches – backstitch for the branches and straight stitch for the leaves.

1.
Find the centre of your linen or cotton evenweave fabric, mark it with a pin (see page 10), and fix it into the appropriate hoop (see page 8): snowflake 1 fits into a 13cm (5in) hoop and snowflakes 2 and 3 fit into the 10cm (4in) hoops.

2.
Using an away waste knot start, stitch your chosen snowflake design (see charts on pages 34–35) from the centre of the chart outwards. If you are new to counted thread embroidery, you can learn about reading charts and preparing your fabric and threads on pages 9–11, and see the Stitch Directory, page 12, for how to work backstitch and straight stitch.

3.
When you have finished the stitching, remove the linen from the hoop. If it is has been positioned off-centre in the hoop, or if it has become creased, you will need to iron it face down over a terry towel before you begin making up. Now position the linen where you want it to lay in the hoop – this will leave a mark on the fabric so that you know where to re-position the linen once the hoop is covered in glue, to prevent you from gluing it in wonky. If you make a mistake with the positioning, re-press and try again.

4.
When you are happy with the position of the linen in the hoop, take it out and put it to one side. Run a thin line of glue all around the outside of the hoop's inner ring, and then place the backing fabric in the hoop, tightening the screw and pulling the fabric taut while the glue is still wet.

{SNOWFLAKE 1 COUNTED THREAD CHART}

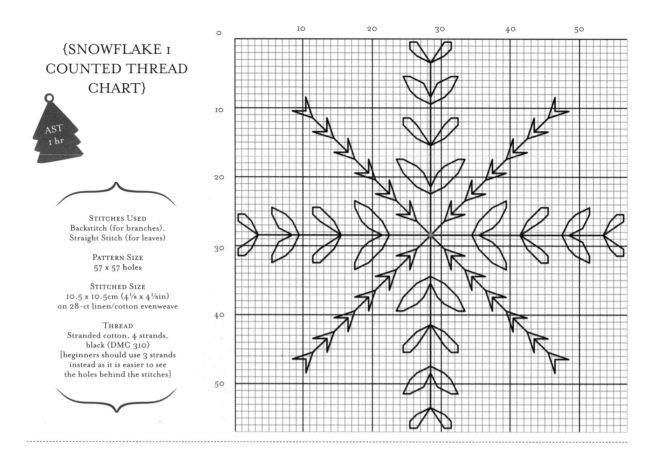

AST 1 hr

STITCHES USED
Backstitch (for branches),
Straight Stitch (for leaves)

PATTERN SIZE
57 x 57 holes

STITCHED SIZE
10.5 x 10.5cm (4⅛ x 4⅛in)
on 28-ct linen/cotton evenweave

THREAD
Stranded cotton, 4 strands,
black (DMC 310)
[beginners should use 3 strands
instead as it is easier to see
the holes behind the stitches]

5.

Leave the glue to dry, and then remove the outer ring. Run another thin line of glue around the inner ring – this time over the top of the backing fabric (see diagram). Sandwich the embroidered linen between the rings, using the mark you left on the fabric as a guide, then tighten the top screw and pull the top layer of fabric taut.

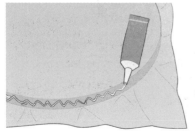

STEP 5

6.

Leave the glue to dry, preferably overnight, and then trim off both layers of excess fabric at the back of the hoop. Keep your scissors flat against the hoop to get the closest cut possible.

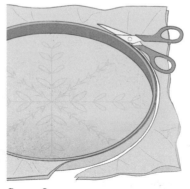

STEP 6

TIPS

◊ Use waste canvas to stitch the snowflakes onto felt and cut them out with pinking shears to make pretty tree decorations.

◊ Try stitching the charts in colourful threads to match the colour palettes of the Merry & Bright or Classic & Cosy sections of this book.

◊ Fill a wall with snowflakes in pale colours and metallic threads to create a magical feel.

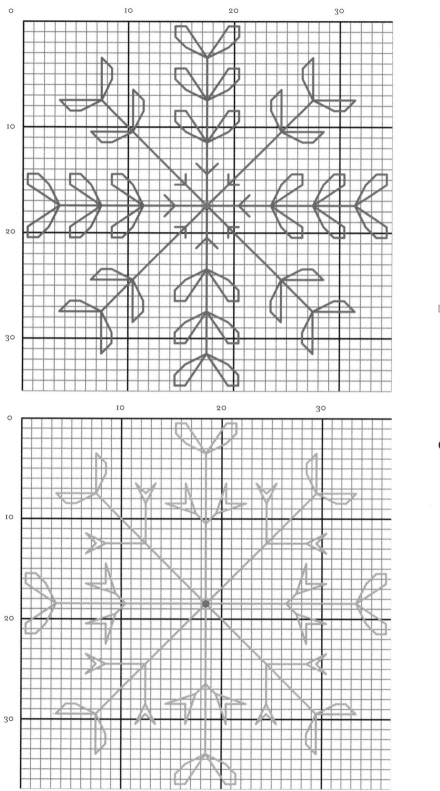

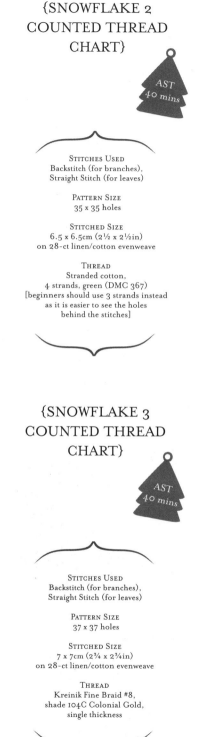

{SNOWFLAKE 2 COUNTED THREAD CHART}

AST
40 mins

STITCHES USED
Backstitch (for branches),
Straight Stitch (for leaves)

PATTERN SIZE
35 x 35 holes

STITCHED SIZE
6.5 x 6.5cm (2½ x 2½in)
on 28-ct linen/cotton evenweave

THREAD
Stranded cotton,
4 strands, green (DMC 367)
[beginners should use 3 strands instead
as it is easier to see the holes
behind the stitches]

{SNOWFLAKE 3 COUNTED THREAD CHART}

AST
40 mins

STITCHES USED
Backstitch (for branches),
Straight Stitch (for leaves)

PATTERN SIZE
37 x 37 holes

STITCHED SIZE
7 x 7cm (2¾ x 2¾in)
on 28-ct linen/cotton evenweave

THREAD
Kreinik Fine Braid #8,
shade 104C Colonial Gold,
single thickness

Mistletoe Snowflake Hoops

{ MERRY & BRIGHT
for modernists }

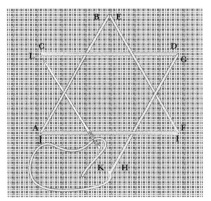

Geometric Gems

{MATERIALS}

FOR EACH GEM

14-count waste canvas, 10 x 10cm (4 x 4in)

Two pieces of thick (1mm/^{1}/$_{16}$in+) 100% wool felt, 10 x 10cm (4 x 4in) each

1.5m (5ft) stranded cotton embroidery thread in colour to contrast felt

Sharp chenille needle, size 18 or 20

Water spray and tweezers

Embroidery scissors and pins

Cotton string, 18cm (7in)

1m (3¼ft) stranded cotton embroidery thread to match felt

Sharp embroidery needle, size 6

Toy stuffing

Mini no-sew frame (10cm/4in side bars and rollers) and masking tape (optional)

Rotary cutter, metal ruler and cutting mat (optional)

These squashy little geometric tree ornaments are magnificently quick to make and pack a mighty punch of colour to brighten up your day. Speedy, simple and seriously stylish – if you are looking for instant stitching gratification, then this is the project for you.

1.

Mark the centre of the waste canvas and attach it to one piece of the felt (see page 6). Tape the layered fabric into the frame if you are using one (see page 7).

2.

Cut a length of stranded cotton (use all six strands), thread onto the chenille needle and tie a double knot in the end of the thread (a knot is used here as there is nowhere on the reverse to secure the thread).

3.

Following the charts on page 41 and counting outwards from the centre, stitch your chosen design in straight stitch (see page 12). The stitches in the diamond design can be worked in any order, but the star looks particularly good stitched in the sequence shown in the diagram below, so that all of the stitches overlap, with the final few stitches in the middle being woven in between each other. Secure thread with another knot at the end.

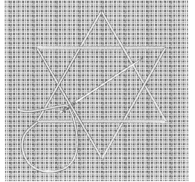

STEP 3

4.

When you have finished stitching, unpick the tacking stitches and remove the waste canvas (see page 6).

5.

Cut a border around the stitched shape approximately 1cm (⅜in) from your stitches – the diamond can be roughly the same shape as your stitching, but the star is best cut into a hexagon around the outer points. I found the easiest way to do this is with a rotary cutter and ruler, but a good eye and a pair of scissors will do the job just as well.

STEP 5

6.

Using the cut shape as a template, cut an identical shape from the second piece of felt. Layer the shapes together with the embroidered piece on top, and sandwich the string, folded into a loop, in between. Pin the layers together.

7.

Using a single strand of embroidery thread at double thickness, chosen to match the colour of the felt, begin with a knotless loop start (see page 10) and join both layers of felt with a small, neat running stitch close to the edge, sewing the loop into place as you go. Before stitching up the final side, fill the shape with toy stuffing.

STEP 7

8.

Continue stitching to close the last side and secure the end of the thread with a couple of backstitches before finishing off (see page 11).

TIPS

◊ *I always err on the side of simplicity, but you can add extra colour and detail by choosing pretty ribbon for your hanging loop.*
◊ *Try using tapestry wool in place of stranded cotton for an extra-chunky look.*
◊ *Add another pop of colour by using contrasting thread to stitch the shape together.*

THREAD COLOURS USED

Diamond: aquamarine (DMC 992) and cream (DMC ecru)

Star: cream (DMC ecru) and neon pink (DMC E1010)

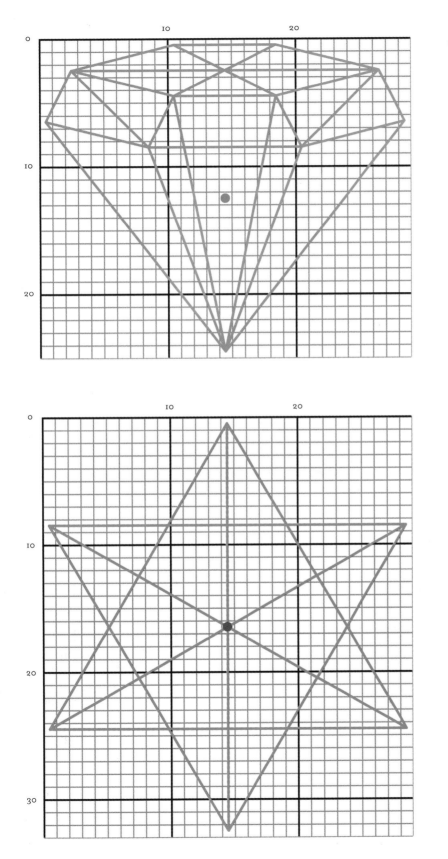

{DIAMOND COUNTED THREAD CHART}

STITCHES USED
Straight Stitch

PATTERN SIZE
29 x 25 holes

STITCHED SIZE
5.5 x 4.5cm (2¼ x 1¾in)
on 14-ct waste canvas

THREAD
Stranded cotton, 6 strands
(not separated), any colour

{STAR COUNTED THREAD CHART}

STITCHES USED
Straight Stitch

PATTERN SIZE
29 x 33 holes

STITCHED SIZE
5.5 x 6cm (2¼ x 2⅜in)
on 14-ct waste canvas

THREAD
Stranded cotton, 6 strands
(not separated), any colour

Perpetual 'Paper' Chain

{MATERIALS}

FOR EACH CHAIN LINK

14-count waste canvas, 25cm (10in) wide (see step 1)

Two pieces of thick (1mm/$\frac{1}{16}$in+) 100% wool felt, 25 x 3cm (10 x 1$\frac{1}{8}$in) each

1.5m (5ft) stranded cotton embroidery thread in colour to contrast felt or 4m (13ft) Kreinik Fine Braid #8, shade 104C Colonial Gold

Sharp embroidery needle, size 6

Embroidery scissors and pins

Water spray and tweezers

Plasticard, 0.5mm thick (20 Thou), 24.5 x 2.5cm (9$\frac{1}{2}$ x 1in) strip

1m (3$\frac{1}{4}$ft) stranded cotton embroidery thread to match felt

Two snap fasteners, 9mm diameter

Ruler and tailor's chalk

Paper scissors or craft knife for cutting Plasticard

Rotary cutter, metal ruler and cutting mat (optional)

Who doesn't love a paper chain? But I hate that I have to throw them away when it's time to take them down – this sturdy felt version solves that little problem. Make it your annual Christmas tradition to add a few links every year. Drape them over a bookshelf, use them in place of tinsel on the tree, or hang them in shapes on the wall to bring a big dollop of jollity to your holiday display in perpetuity.

1.

Cut the strips of felt and Plasticard to size as necessary: the strip of felt should measure 25 x 3cm (10 x 1$\frac{1}{8}$in) and the Plasticard a little smaller at 24.5 x 2.5cm (9$\frac{1}{2}$ x 1in). (If you don't have a rotary cutter, use tailor's chalk and a ruler to mark out strips on felt, then cut out with scissors.) The waste canvas needs to be cut at exactly the same number of holes wide as the chart. To do this, cut a piece of waste canvas that is 25cm (10in) wide (which is the finished length of the strip), then move from one edge to the other, cutting along every 18th hole (see diagram).

2.

Sew a strip of waste canvas to one of the pieces of felt using waste thread and a loose running stitch (see page 12, but note it is not necessary to mark the centre of the waste canvas for this

project). The waste canvas will be slightly larger than the felt, so make sure that there is an even border all around the outside and that the felt is squarely in the middle.

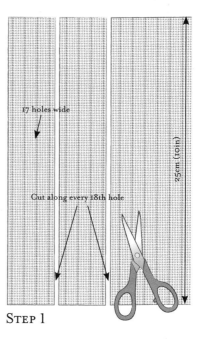

17 holes wide

25cm (10in)

Cut along every 18th hole

STEP 1

3.

This is the one project in the book where you do not count from the centre of the pattern. Because you have cut the waste canvas to the exact width of the chart, you can count the number of holes from one of the corners to the first point of the motif and start stitching from there. The charted designs, pages 46–47, are all stitched with two strands, so use a knotless loop start (see page 10).

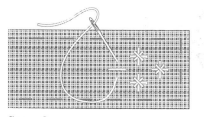

STEP 3

4.

When you have finished stitching your chosen design, unpick the tacking stitches and remove the waste canvas (see page 6).

5.

Using two strands of embroidery thread to match the felt and beginning with a knotless loop start, sew the base parts of two snap fasteners securely to the end of your embroidered strip, about 3cm (1⅛in) from the unembroidered end. Sew the two top parts of the snap fasteners to the very end of the other piece of felt at the same distance apart.

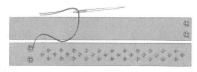

STEP 5

STEP 6

6.

Layer the two strips of felt together so that the snap fasteners are facing out and join by sewing along one end and one side with a small neat running stitch just a few millimetres from the edge, again using two strands of embroidery thread to match the felt. (You can use pins to hold the strips in place, but I just held them together as I went.) Before you start to sew along the third edge, insert the strip of Plasticard – it needs to be a snug fit, but if it is a few millimetres too long, trim a little off the end.

7.

Continue sewing along the last two edges and secure the end of the thread with a couple of backstitches before finishing off (see page 11). Join the snap fasteners to turn the strip into a chain link (the overlap provides extra stability and strength). Make another link to start to form your 'paper' chain.

TIPS

◊ Plasticard has the thickness of card but is made out of plastic, so it holds its shape better and is much more durable. You can cut it with scissors, but it is cleaner and quicker to use a metal ruler and scalpel or craft knife. It is available from craft shops and lots of places online — I bought a pack of 10 sheets very cheaply on eBay.

◊ I cut lots of strips of felt, waste canvas and Plasticard out at the start, so that I didn't have to keep stopping to measure each time I made a new link.

◊ The felt I used is available in 20 x 30cm (8 x 12in) sheets, so you can get six strips (enough for three chain links) out of each sheet. See Suppliers, page 79.

◊ To add extra colour, use a different coloured felt for the inside (back) of the link, or sew the felt strips together with a contrasting coloured thread.

THREAD COLOURS USED
Various combinations of the following:

DMC Stranded Cotton:
cream (ecru),
lime green (166),
khaki (3022),
mint green (564)

DMC Light Effects:
neon pink (E1010)

Kreinik Fine Braid #8,
shade 104C Colonial Gold

{PERPETUAL 'PAPER' CHAIN COUNTED THREAD CHARTS}

STITCHES USED
Straight Stitch
(snowflakes, stags and trees),
Double Straight Cross Stitch
(stars)

PATTERN SIZE
17 x 138 holes

STITCHED SIZE
3 x 25cm (1⅛ x 10in)
on 14-ct waste canvas

THREAD
Stranded cotton,
2 strands any colour
or
Kreinik Fine Braid #8,
shade 104C Colonial Gold,
single thickness

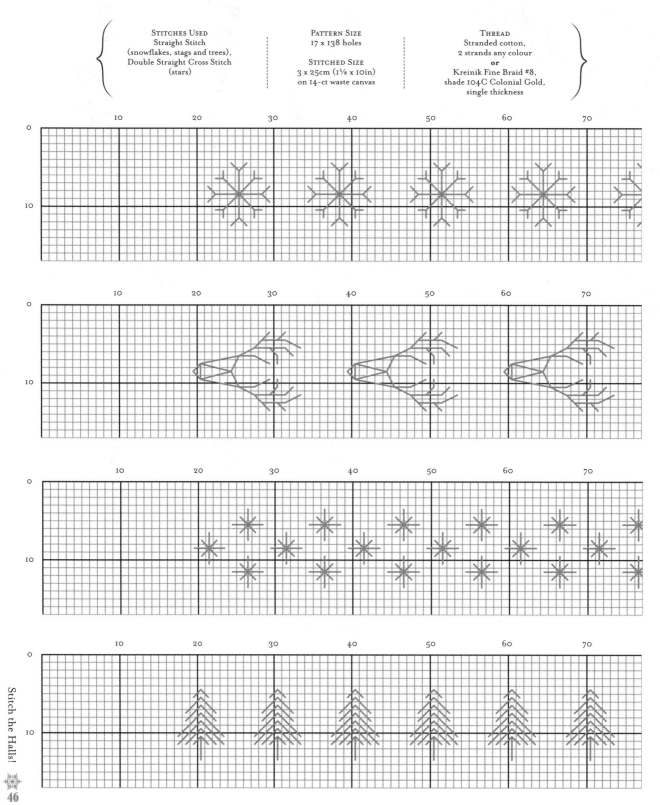

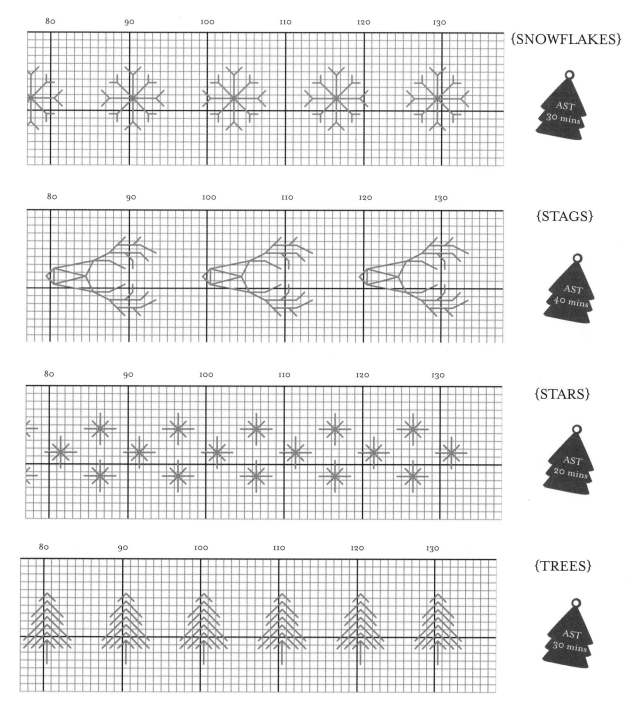

{SNOWFLAKES}

AST
30 mins

{STAGS}

AST
40 mins

{STARS}

AST
20 mins

{TREES}

AST
30 mins

Mini Sampler Stocking

{MATERIALS}

14-count waste canvas, 15 x 20cm (6 x 8in)

Two pieces of thick (1mm/$\frac{1}{16}$in+) cream 100% wool felt, 15 x 20cm (6 x 8in) each

Stranded cotton embroidery thread: 3m (10ft) in bright coral (DMC 3706) and 2m (6$\frac{2}{3}$ft) in aqua (DMC 964)

4m (13ft) Kreinik Fine Braid #8, shade 002 Gold

Sharp embroidery needle, size 6

Embroidery scissors and pins

Water spray and tweezers

Sewing needle and cream thread

Toy stuffing

Cotton tape or ribbon, 15cm (6in)

Pencil or coloured tailor's chalk

Mini no-sew frame (15cm/6in side bars and rollers) and masking tape (optional)

If you haven't tried counted thread embroidery before, then this is the perfect starter project. The simple stripes will help you get used to following a chart and teach you lots of new stitches. It is also quick and easy to make up so if, like me, you prefer stitching to finishing, it's just the ticket.

1.
Mark the centre of the waste canvas and attach it to one piece of the felt (see page 6). Tape the layered fabric into the frame if you are using one (see page 7).

2.
Following the chart on page 51, count outwards from the centre and using an away waste knot start (see page 10), stitch the design one row at a time, aligning all subsequent rows by counting their distance from the ones you have already completed. For how to follow a counted thread chart, see page 9, and for details of the individual stitch techniques, see pages 12–15. Use three strands of the stranded cotton embroidery thread and a single thickness of the metallic thread.

3.
When you have finished stitching, take the fabric out of the frame, unpick the tacking stitches and remove the waste canvas (see page 6).

4.
Use a pencil or tailor's chalk to draw a line approximately 2cm (¾in) outside your stitches (see diagram); cut out the marked stocking shape and use it as a template to cut an identical shape from the second piece of felt. I find the most accurate way to do this is to pin the cut-out embroidery to the other piece of felt and then cut directly around the edge.

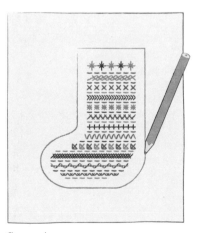

STEP 4

5.

Place the two shapes together with right sides facing out and hold in place with a few pins. Starting at the top left-hand corner and working downwards around the curves, sew the two pieces of felt together with a neat running stitch just a few millimetres from the edge. When you get to the top right-hand corner, remove all of the pins and fill the stocking with toy stuffing (leave the needle threaded ready to close the top edge in step 6).

6.

Take the piece of cotton tape or ribbon and fold it in half to make a hanging loop. Pin the loop in between the two layers with the ends pushed about 1cm (⅜in) inside (see diagram), and then continue the line of running stitch all along the top edge to close the stocking. When you get to the end, secure the thread with a couple of backstitches before finishing off (see page 11).

TIPS

◊ *You could line your mini stocking with some extra felt and leave the top open to be filled with miniature goodies following the making up instructions for the Snowy Forest Mittens (pages 18–20).*

◊ *I have chosen to use felt because it is non-woven and smooth so it really highlights the textures created by all the different stitches, but this design would look great stitched onto linen or evenweave too. If using linen or evenweave, make sure you allow extra for seam allowances.*

◊ *Felt and threads both come in a gazillion colours, so feel free to mix and match to include your favourites.*

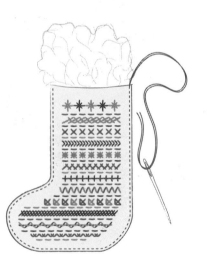

STEP 5

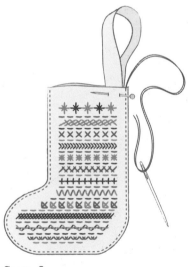

STEP 6

{MINI SAMPLER STOCKING COUNTED THREAD CHART}

STITCHES USED
See chart

PATTERN SIZE
36 x 49 holes

STITCHED SIZE
6.5 x 9cm
(2½ x 3½in)
on 14-ct waste canvas

THREAD
Stranded cotton, 3 strands,
bright coral (DMC 3706)
and
aqua (DMC 964);
Kreinik Fine Braid #8,
shade 002 Gold, single thickness

AST
3 hrs

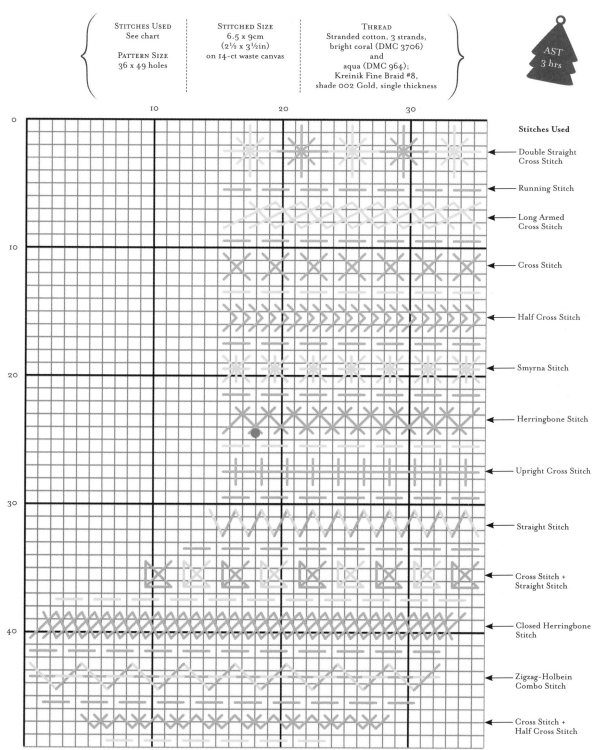

Stitches Used

← Double Straight Cross Stitch

← Running Stitch

← Long Armed Cross Stitch

← Cross Stitch

← Half Cross Stitch

← Smyrna Stitch

← Herringbone Stitch

← Upright Cross Stitch

← Straight Stitch

← Cross Stitch + Straight Stitch

← Closed Herringbone Stitch

← Zigzag-Holbein Combo Stitch

← Cross Stitch + Half Cross Stitch

Advent Tree Bag-lets

I designed the Advent Tree Bag-lets because I live in a tiny little hobbit house that is too small for a real Christmas tree, and because I love pretty advent calendars that are big enough to hold lots of little treats for everyone in the house. You can use temporary hooks or washi tape to artfully arrange these multi-tasking minis on the wall, or dangle them from a collection of twigs, or pin them to a notice board.

{MATERIALS}

FOR EACH BAG

32-count cream linen or cotton evenweave fabric, 15 x 20cm (6 x 8in)

Three pieces of cream cotton backing fabric (calico or craft cotton), 11 x 13cm (4¼ x 5¼in) each

Up to 3m (10ft) stranded cotton embroidery thread or up to 7m

(23ft) Kreinik braid in assorted colours (see charts for details)

Tapestry needles, sizes 24 and 26

Two lengths of cotton tape, 20cm (8in) each

Embroidery scissors and pins

Tracing paper, pencil and paper scissors

Sewing machine or sewing needle and cream sewing thread

Rotary cutter, metal ruler and cutting mat (optional)

Mini no-sew frame (15cm/6in side bars and rollers) and masking tape (optional)

Pinking shears and point turner (optional)

FOR THE ADVENT CALENDAR COLLECTION

To make the entire set of 24 bags I used the following:

Thread

DMC stranded cotton in greens and aqua shades: 1 skein each of 966, 3817, 166, 563, 564, 992

DMC Light Effects: 2 skeins of E1010 (neon pink)

Kreinik Very Fine Braid #4: 1 reel of shade 104C Colonial Gold

Kreinik Fine Braid #8: 1 reel of shade 104C Colonial Gold

Kreinik Medium Braid #16: 1 reel of shade 002 Gold

Cream sewing thread (for making up): 1 reel

Fabric

Zweigart 32-count Murano, shade 0264 ivory, 60 x 140cm (24 x 56in)

2m (80in) of calico for backing and lining

10m (11yd) of 1-cm (⅜-in) wide cotton herringbone tape

1.

Find the centre of your evenweave fabric and mark it with a pin (see page 10); fix it into the frame if you are using one (see page 7).

2.

Stitch your chosen tree design from the centre of the chart outwards, using the thread requirements detailed on the chart (see pages 56–58). If you are new to counted embroidery, you can learn about reading charts and preparing your fabric and threads on pages 9–11, and refer to the Stitch Directory, pages 12–15, for how to work the stitch techniques. After you have completed the tree, stitch the date numbers into the bottom left-hand corner – the rectangular boxes on the chart indicate where to align these.

3.

When you have finished stitching, remove the fabric from its frame and give it a press, placing it face down over a terry towel to protect the stitches.

Now trim your fabric down to 11 x 13cm (4¼ x 5¼in) with the stitching in the centre. To help with alignment, trace the template on page 77 onto a piece of tracing paper and cut it out. Be sure to trace the centre lines onto the template as this will help you to position your stitching in the centre of the shape. Mark the fabric around the template with a pencil and cut it out.

4.

Cut three pieces of cream cotton fabric each measuring 11 x 13cm (4¼ x 5¼in): one for the back of the bag and two for the lining. Pin a 20cm (8in) length of cotton tape to the embroidered front and to the cotton fabric back piece (right sides facing up) to make two downward facing handles (see diagram). The ends of the tape should be level with the edge of the fabric and placed roughly 2cm (¾in) in from the edges.

5.

Layer a lining piece onto the front panel with right sides facing so that the handle is sandwiched in between. Pin together and sew along the top edge with a 1cm (⅜in) seam by hand or machine. (If hand stitching, a backstitch or close running stitch is best.) Attach the second lining piece to the back panel in the same way.

6.

Press the seams open on the joined panels and trim away the excess fabric – pinking shears are great for finishing edges on calico or craft cotton, but it is best to cut the evenweave fabric along the weave line to prevent further fraying (see diagram).

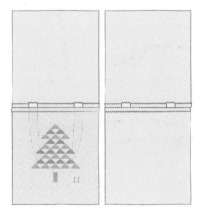

STEP 6

STEP 4

STEP 3

7.

Layer the joined back/lining panel and the joined front/lining panel together with right sides facing, so that the front and back pieces are opposite each other and the two lining pieces are paired up (the handles should be in the middle). Pin the layers together and sew around three edges with a 1cm (⅜in) seam, leaving the lining end open. Press the seams open and trim away the excess fabric as before (see step 6).

8.

Turn the bag out the right way through the gap in the lining and gently push out the corners with a point turner or similar blunt poking tool.

9.

Press the bag with the stitches face down over a terry towel, to remove any creases from turning out. Fold in the raw edges at the open edges of the lining by 1cm (⅜in) and press into place; sew with a neat topstitch as close to the edge as you can get (see diagram).

10.

Push the lining down into the bag and press one final time, paying particular attention to the fold around the top edge.

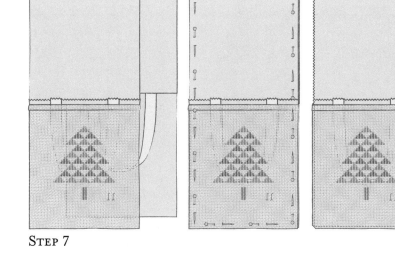

STEP 7

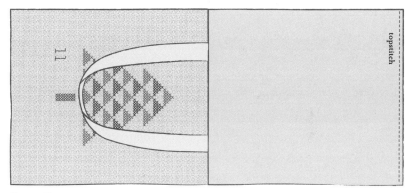

STEP 9

{DATE NUMBERS COUNTED THREAD CHART}

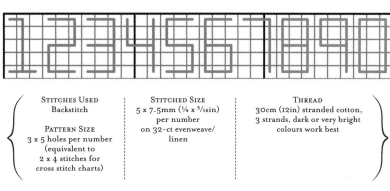

STITCHES USED	STITCHED SIZE	THREAD
Backstitch	5 x 7.5mm (¼ x ⁵⁄₁₆in) per number on 32-ct evenweave/ linen	30cm (12in) stranded cotton, 3 strands, dark or very bright colours work best
PATTERN SIZE 3 x 5 holes per number (equivalent to 2 x 4 stitches for cross stitch charts)		

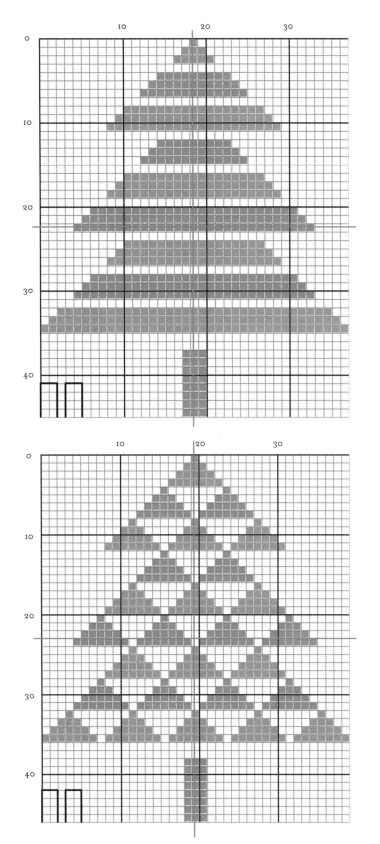

{CHUNKY STRIPES CROSS STITCH CHART}

STITCHES USED
Cross Stitch

PATTERN SIZE
37 x 45 stitches

STITCHED SIZE
6 x 7.5cm (2⅜ x 3in)
on 32-ct evenweave/linen

THREAD
3m (10ft) stranded cotton,
2 strands,
or
7m (23ft) Kreinik
Very Fine Braid #4,
single thickness,
in assorted colours
allocated as you wish

AST
3½ hrs

{TRIANGLES CROSS STITCH CHART}

STITCHES USED
Cross Stitch

PATTERN SIZE
39 x 46 stitches

STITCHED SIZE
6.5 x 7.5cm (2½ x 3in)
on 32-ct evenweave/linen

THREAD
3m (10ft) stranded cotton,
2 strands,
or
7m (23ft) Kreinik
Very Fine Braid #4,
single thickness,
in assorted colours
allocated as you wish

AST
3 hrs

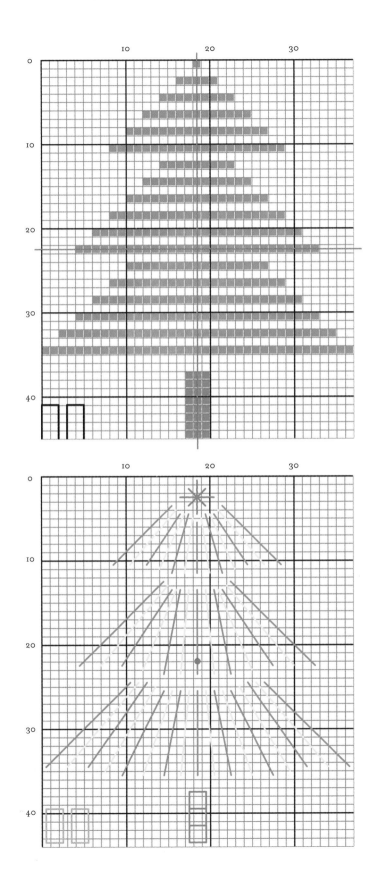

{SKINNY STRIPES CROSS STITCH CHART}

AST
2½ hrs

STITCHES USED
Cross Stitch

PATTERN SIZE
37 x 45 stitches

STITCHED SIZE
6 x 7.5cm (2⅜ x 3in)
on 32-ct evenweave/linen

THREAD
2.5m (8⅓ft) stranded cotton,
2 strands,
or
6m (20ft) Kreinik
Very Fine Braid #4,
single thickness,
in assorted colours
allocated as you wish

{STARBURST COUNTED THREAD CHART}

AST
40 mins

STITCHES USED
Straight Stitch (tree),
Double Straight Cross Stitch (star),
Backstitch (trunk)

PATTERN SIZE
37 x 44 holes

STITCHED SIZE
6.5 x 7.5cm (2½ x 3in)
on 32-ct evenweave/linen

THREAD
2m (6⅔ft) stranded cotton,
3 strands,
or
6m (20ft) Kreinik
Fine Braid #8,
single thickness,
in assorted colours
allocated as you wish

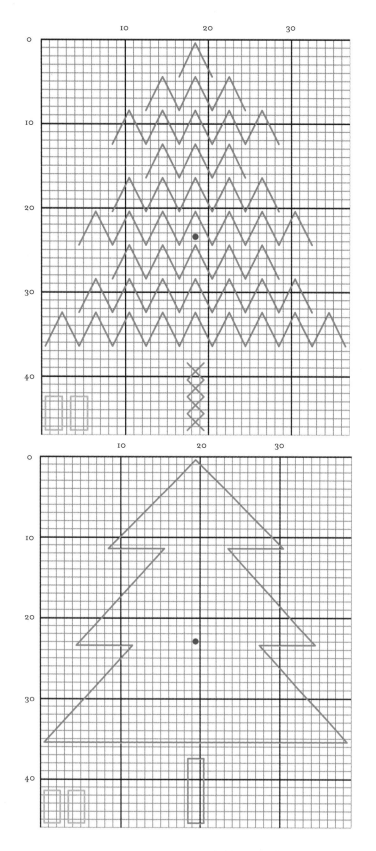

{CHEVRONS COUNTED THREAD CHART}

AST
45 mins

STITCHES USED
Straight Stitch (tree),
Cross Stitch (trunk)

PATTERN SIZE
37 x 47 holes

STITCHED SIZE
6 x 7.5cm (2⅜ x 3in)
on 32-ct evenweave/linen

THREAD
2m (6⅔ft) stranded cotton,
4 strands,
or
3m (10ft) Kreinik
Medium Braid #16,
single thickness,
in assorted colours
allocated as you wish

{BACKSTITCH COUNTED THREAD CHART}

STITCHES USED
Backstitch
(make horizontal
backstitches double length)

PATTERN SIZE
39 x 46 holes

STITCHED SIZE
6.5 x 7.5cm (2½ x 3in)
on 32-ct evenweave/linen

THREAD
1.5m (5ft) stranded cotton,
3 strands,
or
3m (10ft) Kreinik
Fine Braid #8,
single thickness,
in assorted colours
allocated as you wish

AST
30 mins

CLASSIC & COSY
for traditionalists

Tiny Highland Village Garland

{MATERIALS}

FOR EACH COTTAGE

14-count waste canvas, 10 x 10cm (4 x 4in)

Two pieces of thick (1mm/$\frac{1}{16}$in+) cream 100% wool felt, 10 x 10cm (4 x 4in) each

2.5m (8$\frac{1}{3}$ft) stranded cotton embroidery thread in crimson (DMC 816)

Sharp embroidery needle, size 6

Cream sewing thread

Embroidery scissors

Water spray and tweezers

Thick cotton string, for making up garland

Mini no-sew frame (10cm/4in side bars and rollers) and masking tape (optional)

Two of my greatest loves are Christmas and the Scottish Highlands – put them together and you have a sweet little village garland. The simple motif is easy to stitch, and a great introduction to fractional cross stitches. The garland is also a doddle to make up, so all in all you can't go wrong.

1.

Mark the centre of the waste canvas and attach it to one piece of the felt (see page 6). Tape the layered fabric into the frame if you are using one (see page 7).

2.

Following the chart on page 64, count outwards from the centre and using an away waste knot start (see page 10), stitch the design in rows, using three strands of embroidery thread.

3.

When you have finished stitching, take the fabric out of the frame, unpick the tacking stitches and remove the waste canvas (see page 6).

4.

Use embroidery scissors to cut carefully around your embroidery, about 5mm (¼in) from the edge of your stitches. Use the cut-out house as a template to cut a duplicate shape from the remaining piece of felt.

5.

Secure a single strand of cream sewing thread behind some existing stitches on the back of the embroidered house, place the house shapes together, right sides facing out, and begin sewing together, from the base of the roof, with a very fine running stitch worked directly alongside the edge of your embroidery stitches (they should be virtually invisible), stitching to the other side but leaving the roof open.

STEP 5

6.

Cut a piece of thick cotton string
at least as long as you want your
garland to be and thread it between
the open layers of the roof (leaving
a 50cm/20in tail on the string for
hanging), then continue to neatly
stitch the roof together, sandwiching
the string inside. Secure the thread
with a couple of backstitches before
finishing off (see page 11).

7.

Repeat steps 1–6 until you have added
the number of houses you want to
complete your garland. I arranged
mine every 4cm (1½in) but feel
free to experiment with the spacing.
Remember to leave a 50cm (20in) tail
on the string for hanging after you
have placed your final house.

TIPS

◊ *Stitch the houses in lots of different colours
to give your village a little variety.*

◊ *Try out different yarns and twines to string
your houses from — weightier options will give a
nice drape to your garland.*

◊ *Turn the tiny houses into individual
decorations by stitching a hanging loop between
the layers.*

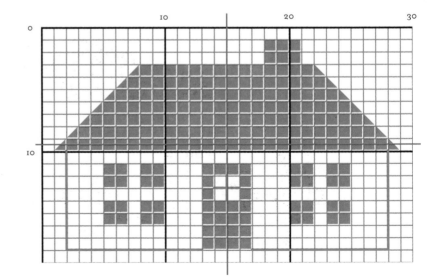

{TINY HIGHLAND COTTAGE CROSS STITCH CHART}

STITCHES USED
Cross Stitch,
Three-Quarter Cross Stitch,
Backstitch (outline),
Straight Stitch (in door)

PATTERN SIZE
30 x 19 stitches

STITCHED SIZE
5.5 x 3.5cm (2¼ x 1⅜in)
on 14-ct waste canvas

THREAD
Stranded cotton,
3 strands,
crimson (DMC 816)

His & Hers Christmas Jumpers

Christmas just wouldn't be the same without an embarrassing array of outlandish knitwear. I have recently learned to knit but have yet to graduate to making actual clothing, so I made these miniature jumpers to satisfy my craving for a human-size one. They make wonderful Christmas cards, but are also particularly adorable when hung from little bits of wire fashioned into teeny-weeny coat hangers.

{MATERIALS}

FOR EACH JUMPER

14-count waste canvas, 15 x 15cm (6 x 6in)

Thick (1mm/¹⁄₁₆in+) 100% wool felt in assorted colours, 15 x 15cm (6 x 6in) each

4m (13ft) stranded cotton embroidery thread in assorted colours

Sharp embroidery needle, size 6

Embroidery scissors and pins

Water spray and tweezers

Tracing paper, pencil and paper scissors

C6 greetings card blank and craft glue

Mini no-sew frame (15cm/6in side bars and rollers) and masking tape (optional)

1.
Mark the centre of the waste canvas and attach it to the felt (see page 6). Tape the layered fabric into the frame if you are using one (see page 7).

2.
Following your chosen jumper chart on page 67, count outwards from the centre and using an away waste knot start (see page 10), stitch the design in rows, using three strands of embroidery thread. Take care not to carry any threads from the middle of the body to the arms as the fabric in between them will eventually be cut.

3.
When you have finished stitching, take the fabric out of the frame, unpick the tacking stitches and remove the waste canvas (see page 6).

4.
Transfer the relevant template (page 78) to a piece of tracing paper and pin it to your embroidery, making sure that none of the stitches is too close to the edge, then cut carefully around the template using embroidery scissors. You can use the template as a guide and adapt the jumper shape as you wish.

STEP 4

5.
Cover the back of the cut-out jumper with craft glue and stick it to the front of the card blank.

TIPS

◊ *To make your jumper into a hanging decoration, cut an identically shaped piece of felt for the backing, then glue or stitch the two layers together, sandwiching either a hanging loop or a mini coat hanger in between.*

◊ *Make your own mini coat hangers from fine wire, or find ready-made versions in the dolls' house section of craft shops or search online.*

◊ *Christmas jumpers are full of colour and often seriously over the top, so this is the perfect opportunity to use up some of the little bits of thread kicking about in your sewing box to make your own festive colour combination.*

THREAD COLOURS USED

His dark grey jumper:
cream (DMC ecru),
bright green (DMC 505),
grey-green (DMC 926)

His red jumper:
golden olive (DMC 832),
bright green (DMC 505),
cream (DMC ecru)

Her cream jumper:
light green (DMC 524),
bright green (DMC 505),
grey-green (DMC 926)

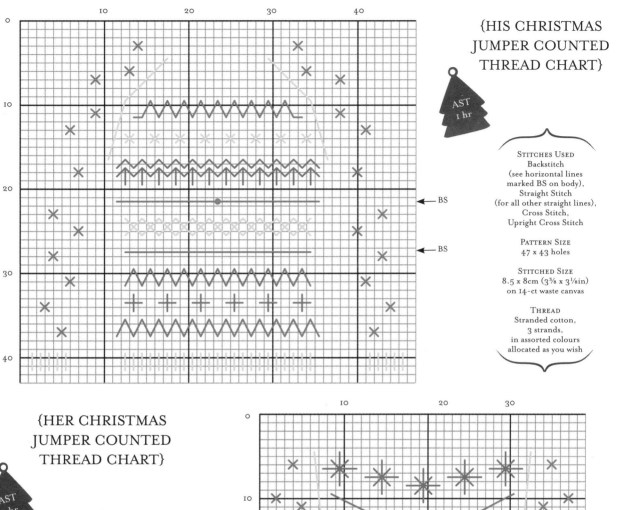

AST
1 hr

← BS

← BS

STITCHES USED
Backstitch
(see horizontal lines
marked BS on body),
Straight Stitch
(for all other straight lines),
Cross Stitch,
Upright Cross Stitch

PATTERN SIZE
47 x 43 holes

STITCHED SIZE
8.5 x 8cm (3⅜ x 3⅛in)
on 14-ct waste canvas

THREAD
Stranded cotton,
3 strands,
in assorted colours
allocated as you wish

{HER CHRISTMAS
JUMPER COUNTED
THREAD CHART}

AST
1 hr

STITCHES USED
Backstitch
(see horizontal lines
marked BS on body),
Straight Stitch
(for all other straight lines),
Cross Stitch,
Double Straight Cross Stitch

PATTERN SIZE
39 x 42 holes

STITCHED SIZE
7.5 x 8cm (3 x 3⅛in)
on 14-ct waste canvas

THREAD
Stranded cotton,
3 strands,
in assorted colours
allocated as you wish

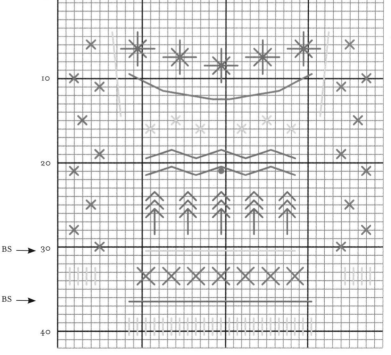

BS →

BS →

His & Hers Christmas Jumpers

Miss Prance-a-Lot Peg Doll

{MATERIALS}

32-count cream linen or cotton evenweave fabric, 15 x 25cm (6 x 10in)

5m (16½ft) stranded cotton embroidery thread in crimson (DMC 816)

Tapestry needle, size 26

Wooden peg doll and 3mm metal ring 'eye' screw

Paints for face and scrap of wool roving for hair

2m (6⅔) embroidery thread in flesh colour (DMC 951)

5m (16½ft) tapestry wool in red (DMC 7108)

Chenille needle, size 16, and sharp embroidery needle, size 6

Electric drill, metal wire and small pliers

Craft glue, embroidery scissors and pins

Sewing machine or fine sewing needle and cream sewing thread

Mini no-sew frame (15cm/6in side bars and 30cm/12in rollers) and masking tape (optional)

Peg dolls are about as traditional as you can possibly get, and yet Miss Prance-a-Lot considers herself a bit of a fashionista. Never seen without her obligatory red lips and beehive, she likes nothing better than dancing the night away with a host of equally glamorous friends. Hang her from a branch and she will show you her moves every time you pass by.

I.
Drill a small hole in the peg for the arms, making the hole just above the point where the body starts to taper into the neck.

2.
Paint on eyes and a mouth to make your peg doll's face. When the paint has dried, screw the 'eye' screw into the top of the peg – this will provide a strong point from which to hang the doll. The screw can be twisted in by hand.

3.
Find the centre of your evenweave fabric and mark it with a pin (see page 10); fix it into the frame if you are using one (see page 7). Following the chart on page 71 and using a knotless loop start (page 10), stitch the design from the centre outwards using two strands of embroidery thread.

4.
Once the stitching is complete press the excess fabric at the bottom of the design (approx 5mm/¼in beneath the row of large cross stitches) to the reverse to form a deep hem. Trim the left- and right-hand edges of the fabric to 1cm (⅜in) from the stitches.

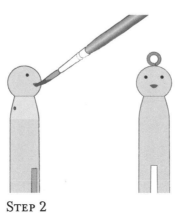

STEP 2

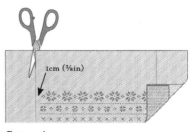

1cm (⅜in)

STEP 4

Miss Prance-a-Lot Peg Doll

❄
69

5.

Open up the pressed hem and pin the two ends of the fabric together so that the right sides are facing and the stitches are running in bands around the middle. Sew along the edge with a 1cm (⅜in) seam. Press the seam open and turn out the right way. Now fold the hem back up along the crease made earlier, re-pressing the edge if needed. Lay the fabric tube next to your peg doll with the folded hem at the point you want your skirt to finish, and cut off the top of the tube where it comes into line with the tapered neck (see diagram).

STEP 5

TIPS

◊ *If you don't have access to an electric drill, search online for pegs with pre-drilled (arm) holes.*

◊ *Wool roving makes very realistic hair and it is available in small quantities from craft shops. Tapestry wool will also work for hair, and as there are often more colour choices, if you are after a specific shade, it may be worth experimenting with that instead.*

◊ *If you prefer, you can try using a pipe cleaner instead of wire for the arms.*

6.

To make the arms, cut a piece of wire 12cm (4¾in) long, push it through the drilled hole and use pliers to curl the ends to form hands. Wrap flesh-coloured embroidery thread around the bottom half of each arm and hand to cover all the wire, adding a dab of glue at the tip of the hand to prevent the thread slipping off. Secure the end of the embroidery thread by using your tapestry needle or a sharp embroidery needle to make a couple of backstitches through the wrapped thread, and then snip off the excess.

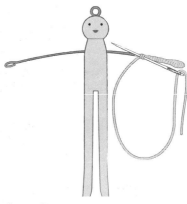

STEP 6

7.

Slip the skirt onto the peg doll. To shape the skirt, arrange folds in the top edge (both back and front) and pin them in place. Wrap a few rounds of tapestry wool tightly around the peg doll's middle to hold the skirt in place and, when it is secure, remove the pins (see diagram).

STEP 7

8.

Continue to wrap wool around the peg doll's top half, working your way down the arms and back up again, until the wood and wire are completely covered and you are happy with the shape. Secure the end of the wool by using the chenille needle to thread it behind the densely wrapped yarn: push the needle through, pull the yarn tight and then trim off the excess length.

STEP 8

9.

Add a blob of glue to the peg doll's head and then wrap a piece of wool roving around the metal ring (from front to back) to look like hair. Take another length of roving and use more glue to stick it to the head, wrapping it in the opposite direction (from back to front) around the ring to cover as much of the 'scalp' as possible, adding further layers if needed. Once the glue has dried, you can twist the wool into a hairstyle to cover the metal ring.

10.

Finally, take the sewing needle or a sharp embroidery needle and a piece of strong sewing thread and use a knotless loop start to attach it through the metal loop of the 'eye' screw (see diagram). Pull the knotless loop tight (it should mostly disappear into the hair) and tie a knot in the ends at the top to create a fine hanging loop. Now just bend the peg doll's arms into shape and she's ready to go!

STEP 10

{SKIRT CROSS STITCH CHART}

STITCHES USED	STITCHED SIZE
Cross Stitch, Running Stitch	15.5 x 6.5cm (6⅛ x 2½in)
PATTERN SIZE	THREAD
98 x 40 stitches	Stranded cotton, 2 strands, crimson (DMC 816)

AST
3 hrs

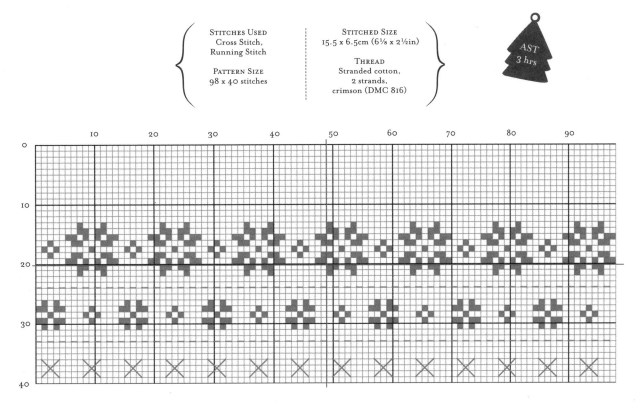

Jumbo Christmas Sock-ing

{MATERIALS}

14-count waste canvas, 35 x 40cm (13¾ x 15¾in)

Four pieces of thick (1mm/¹⁄₁₆in+) dark red 100% wool felt, 35 x 40cm (13¾ x 15¾in) each

Tapestry wool: 4m (13ft) in dark red (DMC 7110) and 6m (20ft) in cream (DMC 7510)

Sharp chenille needle, size 16

Embroidery scissors and pins

Water spray and tweezers

Heavy duty cotton tape, 35cm (13¾in)

Sewing needle and sewing thread to match felt

Tracing paper, pencil and paper scissors

Tailor's chalk

25cm (10in) embroidery hoop

TIP

◊ *Although very easy to make up, some serious counting when stitching makes this best suited if you have some embroidery experience.*

Thick, handmade socks are one of my favourite things in the world, so when I thought about making a stocking, I knew instantly where my inspiration would come from. My sock-ing is designed with serious strength in mind, so you can fill it to the brim with presents and it won't founder.

1.
Mark the centre of the waste canvas and attach it to one piece of the felt (see page 6). Fix the layered fabric into the hoop if you are using one (see page 7).

2.
The pattern for this project is very simple, but because the stitches are worked over three blocks rather than the usual one block, there is quite a bit of maths involved, which could be quite confusing for beginners. Basically, it is like working on linen, except that you need to count in increments of three rather than two. Individual crosses are marked on top of the blocks on the chart on pages 74–75 to help you keep track of the counting.

3.
Work the stitches from the centre of the chart outwards, exactly as you would do with normal cross stitch (see pages 10 and 13), counting from section to section, using a single thickness of the tapestry wool. If you are using a hoop, move it around to get to different areas, especially near the edges.

4.
When you have finished stitching, take the fabric out of the hoop, unpick the tacking stitches and remove the waste canvas (see page 6 – I found it easier to remove the vertical threads first for this project). Iron the embroidered panel face down over a terry towel to remove any hoop creases.

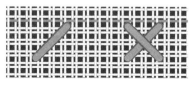

STEP 2

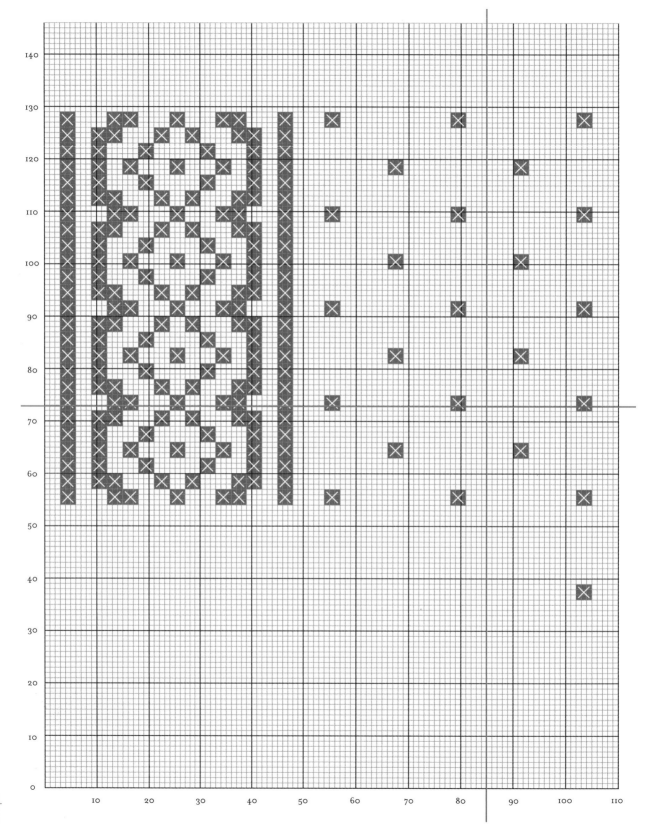

{JUMBO CHRISTMAS SOCK-ING CROSS STITCH CHART}

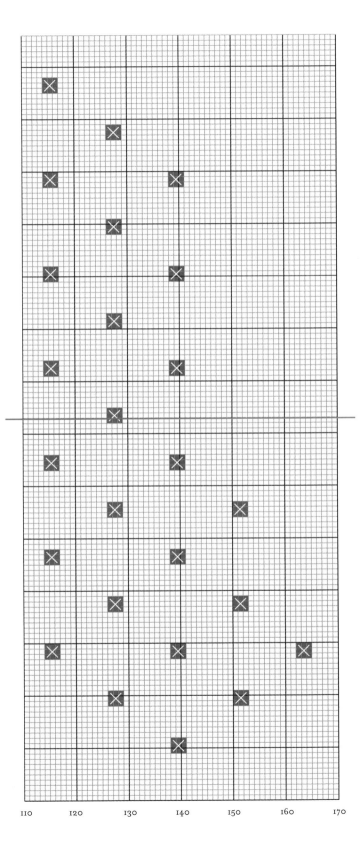

AST
2 hrs

STITCHES USED
Cross Stitch*

PATTERN SIZE
146 x 170 stitches

STITCHED SIZE
26.5 x 31cm (10½ x 12⅜in)

THREAD
Tapestry wool,
dark red (DMC 7110) and
cream (DMC 7510),
single thickness

EXTRA INFO
*The cross stitches are worked
over blocks of 3 x 3 to create
very large crosses; the individual
crosses are marked on top of the
blocks to aid counting

TIPS

◊ *The look of this stocking will differ greatly
depending on the colours you choose, so you can make
one for every member of the family and they will all
look different.*

◊ *Add an extra pop of colour by using contrasting
coloured felt for the lining.*

5.

Draw a sock shape around the edge of the stitches, working by eye or using the template on page 78. If using the template, photocopy it at 200% and then transfer it to tracing paper. Lay the tracing paper over the felt, looking through it to align the stitches evenly inside the template; mark around the edge with tailor's chalk and cut out the shape.

6.

Use the cut-out sock to cut three identical shapes from the remaining three pieces of felt for backing. Take the cotton tape and pin one end of

it at a slight angle in between the embroidered shape and one of the backing pieces. Use a double thickness of sewing thread and a knotless loop start to sew the two pieces together, right sides facing out, along the top edge. To make a strong seam that looks neat on both sides of the fabric, first work a running stitch in one direction and then work your way back to fill in the spaces in between (see diagram). Do a few extra stitches over the hanging loop to hold it firmly in place and secure the ends of the thread with a few backstitches before finishing off (see page 11).

7.

Repeat step 6 to join the other end of the hanging loop between the remaining two felt sock shapes (the tape joins the paired up socks – see diagram), first pinning, then stitching in place along the top edge.

STEP 7

8.

Place the sock back and front together; pin into place and sew all around the edge (through four layers) using double running stitch (see step 6), making sure to leave the top open or there will be nowhere to put the presents! Secure the end of the thread with a couple of backstitches before finishing off.

STEP 6

Templates

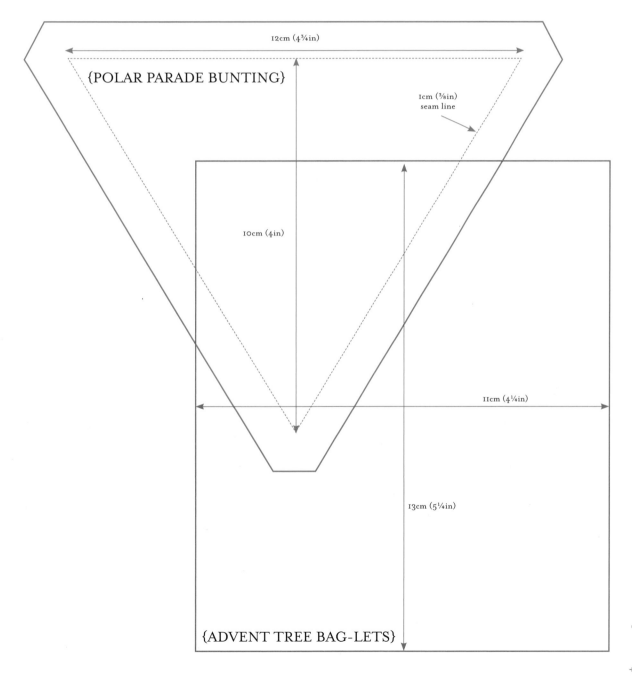

12cm (4¾in)

{POLAR PARADE BUNTING}

1cm (⅜in)
seam line

10cm (4in)

11cm (4¼in)

13cm (5¼in)

{ADVENT TREE BAG-LETS}

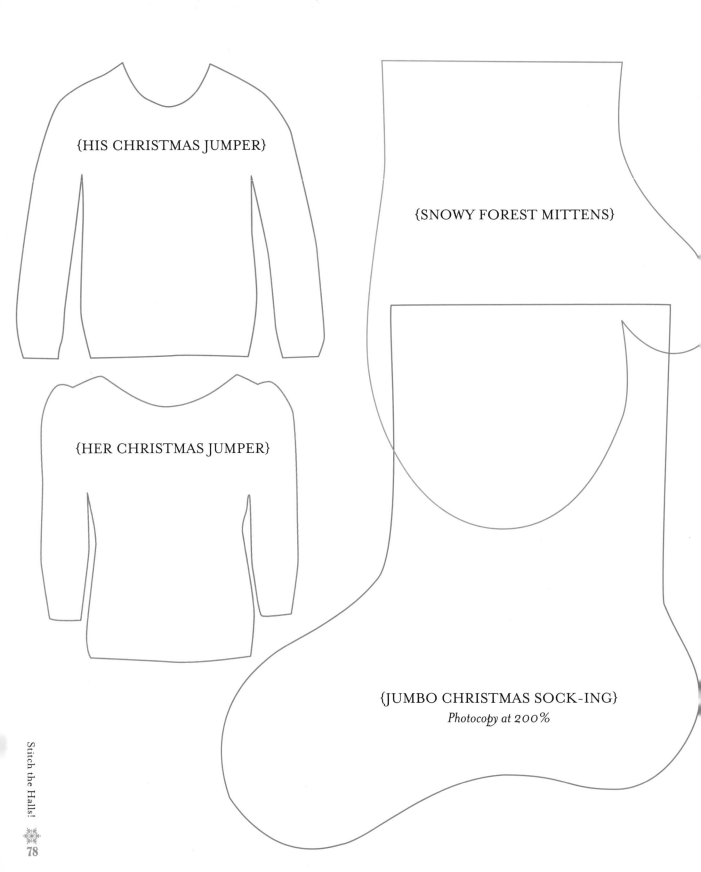

{HIS CHRISTMAS JUMPER}

{SNOWY FOREST MITTENS}

{HER CHRISTMAS JUMPER}

{JUMBO CHRISTMAS SOCK-ING}
Photocopy at 200%

{Suppliers}

{WHAT DELILAH DID}
Contemporary cross stitch and
embroidery patterns, kits, supplies
and accessories.
www.whatdelilahdid.com

SEW AND SO
Massive range of evenweave fabrics,
threads and accessories. Quick,
reliable service.
www.sewandso.co.uk

WOOL FELT COMPANY
100% wool felt, excellent quality
and lovely colours.
www.woolfeltcompany.co.uk

JOHN JAMES NEEDLES
Specialists in embroidery needles –
all types, including easy-threading
versions. www.jjneedles.com

SIESTA FRAMES
Mini no-sew frames, embroidery
hoops and accessories.
www.siestaframes.com

HOBBYCRAFT
Assorted craft supplies, haberdashery
and notions – wool roving, toy
stuffing, greetings card blanks, bias
tape, tracing paper and more.
www.hobbycraft.co.uk

SEWING ONLINE
Snap fasteners, coloured tailor's
chalks and assorted notions.
www.sewing-online.com

THE QUILTED BEAR
Great range of rotary cutters,
rulers and cutting mats.
www.quiltedbear.co.uk

**THE LITTLE CRAFTY
BUGS COMPANY**
Dolly pegs, metal 'eye' screws and
paints. www.littlecraftybugs.co.uk

EBAY
Plasticard, cotton tape/webbing –
especially good for small quantities
of specialist supplies. www.ebay.co.uk

ORGANIC TEXTILE COMPANY
Large selection of organic and fair
trade fabrics. Especially good for
plain cotton backing fabrics.
www.organiccotton.biz

LIBERTY
Nice haberdashery department,
lots of kits and trimmings.
www.liberty.co.uk

{About the Author}

Sophie Simpson

Sophie Simpson (aka
Delilah) is the creator behind
embroidery business, What
Delilah Did. She runs a
successful blog and online
shop where she sells her
distinctive embroidery designs
to customers all over the
world, and her kits are sold in
boutique haberdasheries and
lifestyle shops throughout the United Kingdom.

When she is not making books or dreaming up things for her
own business, Sophie can be found designing projects for the
likes of *Mollie Makes* and *CrossStitcher* magazines. Her designs,
which are a thoroughly modern take on traditional techniques,
are attracting a whole new generation to this age-old craft.
A mildly eccentric girl with a rather overactive imagination,
Sophie lives in a sleepy market town in Norfolk, England
and loves folk music, period dramas, whales and all things
handmade. You can follow her crafty adventures at
www.whatdelilahdid.com.
Other books by Sophie Simpson:
Storyland Cross Stitch, 2013

Acknowledgements

First and foremost I would like to say a big and heartfelt thank you to all of you who bought my last book, as you are the reason I got the chance to make another one. The eldest of my three younger sisters was offended that she didn't get a name check and personal note of thanks in the last book, so Emily, Cassia and Jasmine – this one is for you! Thank you all for the little helping hands you have provided over the past few years. The roast dinner you drove to my house was of course the most important of all, Emily.

Thank you to Lucy for coming to my aid when I was panicking at the eleventh hour, and to my friends and family for putting up with my frequent absence as I worked to follow my dreams. And last but by no means least, to David: for all the punched corners and early morning craft fair set-ups, for your endless patience and for being there whenever I need you. You are a good egg.

First published in the United Kingdom in 2014 by
Pavilion Books Company Limited
1 Gower Street
London
WC1E 6HD

Distributed in the United States and Canada by
Sterling Publishing Co, 387 Park Avenue South,
New York, NY 10016-8810, USA

ISBN 978-1-90939-784-2

A CIP catalogue record for this book is available from the British Library.

OCLC
1/7/2015

10 9 8 7 6 5 4 3 2 1

Reproduction by Mission, Hong Kong
Printed by 1010 Printing International Ltd, China

This book can be ordered direct from
the publisher at www.pavilionbooks.com

Photography by Rachel Whiting
Step-by-step illustrations by Kuo Kang Chen
Decorative illustrations by Ana Victoria Calderón